PASSION

THE ENERGY THAT FUELS LOVE, LIFE, & SPIRITUAL INTIMACY

Lorenza James

Copyright © 2021 by Lorenza James

All rights reserved. This book or any portion thereof may not be reproduced or used in any manner whatsoever without the express written permission of the publisher except for the use of brief quotations in a book review or scholarly journal.

Scripture quotations taken from The Holy Bible, King James Version, Cambridge, 1769.

First Printing: 2021

ISBN (Paperback): 978-1-7372734-0-0
ISBN (E-Book): 978-1-7372734-1-7

Library of Congress Control Number: 2021915635

Cover Design by Daneja Graphix
Book Interior Design by Greater Works Enterprises

Greater Works Enterprises
Website: www.greaterworksenterprises.com

PREFACE

Love, life, and spiritual intimacy are the pursuits human beings long to find and personally explore for happiness and self-fulfillments. Far too many people have settled into living their lives in corners that provide them little joy and no fervent expectations for greeting each day for change or changes that will take them out of the hole they live in. Love without passion is empty expressions, or hollow sounds, or deceptive emotions. Every person desires to be loved, to feel wanted, needed, and desired. Passion keeps romance in relationships, mends hearts together, and gives life to lifeless expressions of love. Equally so, life needs passion. Passion directs your life to careers that keep your interests, and causes you to invest your valued time, and energize your purpose to do what you like to do. Passion becomes your life dedicated to a welcomed work schedule that you dare not miss, delay, or avoid. Ultimately, spiritual intimacy is heightened by passionate love for God and a willing spirit to acknowledge His presence in your life. Praises that draw others into your worship are saturated with a spiritual passion that verifies to others that God is real. Finally, passion is the active force that every person needs as a motivating factor in their lives to achieve their dreams, to enjoy their work, and expressions from a heart of genuine love for God and people.

ACKNOWLEDGEMENTS

I would like to dedicate this book to all my family, friends, and encouragers, and those that have allowed me to share their journeys through the story of their lives.

First, to my family whom I love dearly, and pray constantly for them. My wife Deborah, who has given so much of herself to ensure my success, I give thanks. After 47 years of marriage, I can still count on her to be at my side, to cover my back, and to help me walk forward with purpose and determination. To our five children, Lorenza II (Atom), Michael, Rachael, Amy, and Matthew, I feel blessed by God that you are our children. I value and appreciate each of you. I am thankful for our seven grandchildren: Lorenza III, Keiamber, Michael II, Alexis, Makenna, Matthew II, and Zoe. I am thankful for two outstanding sons-in-law: Andre

Harris (Rachael), and Jeremiah Brown (Amy). Special thanks are extended posthumously to Mrs. Ruby Bennett for helping me to give academic structure to my materials. A great thanks to Rev. David Bennett for his constant encouragement. Additional thanks to numerous friends and well-wishers, including Mrs. Maxine D. Abrams, Mrs. Mamie Reed, and Mrs. Veronica Williams. I appreciate you all.

Table of Contents

PREFACE v
ACKNOWLEDGEMENTS vii

PART I 1
   INTRODUCTION - DOING WHAT YOU LIKE DOING WITH PASSION 2
   CHAPTER 1 - PASSIONATE LOVE 18
   CHAPTER 2 - TRUE LOVE VERSUS FALSE LOVE 21
   CHAPTER 3 - DOING MARRIAGE WITH PASSION 24
   CHAPTER 4 - PASSIONATE LOVE RELATIONSHIPS 33
   CHAPTER 5 - "I LOVE MY HUSBAND" 36
   CHAPTER 6 - THE QUIET STREAM 41

PART II 49
   CHAPTER 7 - LIFE PURSUITS AND SPIRITUAL PASSION 50
   CHAPTER 8 - SPIRITUAL PASSION FOR GOD'S PLAN 56
   CHAPTER 9 - WORKING TO REBUILD A WALL 62
   CHAPTER 10 - A WOMAN NAMED DEVON 71
   CHAPTER 11 - DEBORAH, A WOMAN OF GREAT DEDICATION 84
   CHAPTER 12 - VISION FOR A CITY 92
   CHAPTER 13 - RICHARD AND VICKI (GOSPEL SUPPLY HOUSE) 96

PART III 110
CHAPTER 14 - THE CHURCH AND PASSION 111
CHAPTER 15 - SPIRITUAL LEADERSHIP 116
CHAPTER 16 - THE SPARK AND THE FIRE 128
CHAPTER 17 - ABRAHAM, THE FRIEND OF GOD 136
CHAPTER 18 - MEN GOD TRUSTED 143

PART IV 157
CHAPTER 19 - CONCLUSION 158
CHAPTER 20 - VESTAL GOODMAN AND SQUIRE PARSONS 160
CHAPTER 21 - BOBBY COX 162
CHAPTER 22 - MY FRIEND ALBERT 164
CHAPTER 23 – JOCQUELINE 167
CHAPTER 24 - FINAL THOUGHTS 171

ABOUT THE AUTHOR 173

PART I

INTRODUCTION
DOING WHAT YOU LIKE DOING WITH PASSION

Living life with passion is doing what you like doing! Whether it involves your career, an unfulfilled dream, a love relationship, or a quest that takes you to self-appreciation and fulfilled self-identity. However, having the courage and willingness to pursue such a passionate life requires such personal elements as commitment, dedication, and sacrifice that will enforce and reinforce your path-walk towards reaching and achieving these goals! Passionate motivation brings enthusiasm and opportunities each day that makes every moment valuable, and every experience a well-lived expression of your passion.

This passion is a driving force that leads to personal completion and satisfaction. This kind of passion wakes you up each morning to get the best out of you. This kind of passion is not borrowed emotions or false enthusiasm. It is the kind of passion, in you, that causes you to do what you like doing because it makes you happy doing it. However, without this motivating passion, a person's life often lacks enthusiasm, motivation, and excitement. Without motivating passion, people surrender their lives to complacency towards their jobs, various relationships, and situations that they do regularly, routinely, and often without passion for what they are doing.

Life is a short measurement that's lodged between birth and death. However, what is done during this time determines, to varying degrees, whether you love the life live, and/or whether you value each moment it provides. We understand that value is a subjective goal. A phrase often alluded is one man's trash is another man's treasure. Therefore, the wisest definition of value, for me, is found in the Bible, Matthew 6:21, "For where your treasure is, there will your heart be also," (KJV). Passion for life is found in expectations.

Doing what you like to do is a gratifying way to live. Doing what you like with passion is a fulfilling way to live. One day, as I sat alone in my office at the church where I serve as pastor, I thought about how quickly time passes; how swiftly the years go by. If I had to live that time over again, there is very little that I would change; except perhaps try to live them with the motivating passion it takes to enjoy each moment more. As revealing for me this moment was, I thought and said to myself, "life is too short to live it aimlessly!" I am convinced that life's fulfillment demands that we value each moment by spending our time doing what we truly enjoy doing!

However, far too many people fail to stay focused on the dreams and goals that started their journeys. Such people usually have become discouraged by their life circumstances and situations that derailed their initial motivation. Therefore, they have substituted heartfelt dreams that once called them to live motivated by the passion to achieve and the drive to succeed, to instead find comfort in safe living, or lazy living because it's easier to get through life playing it safe. To live life with passion is akin to living with a divine calling or purpose. I believe that this divine calling should be like fire within that motivates us to do our life's work at its highest level, even if we did not get paid for doing it.

Before you get upset and refuse to read any further, don't give up on this thesis, or misunderstand me! I am not saying that money should not be part of your passion or motivation, nor am I suggesting that anyone should make his/her life a living contribution or monetary donation to the society. Everyone that works should get paid his/her worth based on the works done. What I am saying, though, is that money should not be the top priority or first reason for choosing your life's work. Fulfillment needs to be found in the passion one has for doing every day what he/she likes doing best.

I believe that without passion inspiring the works you do life becomes a series of routine activities that robotically move us from one day to the next. In our efforts to define who we are and give meaning to what we do, we end up structuring our worlds in ways that bring and maintain order for us. We develop habits, schedules, and other personal ways that make life meaningful to us. Habitually, without passion, the average person greets each day's demands by either working at a job, going to a school, taking care of a family, or sitting around wondering about the meaning of life. Such routines often leave negative influences on the way you live, and with the conclusion that life is but a dull, lifeless process.

During this process, people lacking passion often face each day regretting their jobs, regretting having to go to school, regretting having to assume personal or family responsibility, and regretting the living conditions they feel forced to live in. Without passion, there is little motivation to do more than survive the daily routine. Without passion, life becomes a soap opera with a sad refrain of pretending to be happy, to still have dreams and goals, while pretending that you are looking forward to the next day! People that share this dismal view of life sometimes experience great periods of depressions, disappointments, defeats, and even death. Enough is enough! Away with the negatives! On with the positives!

In reaching toward higher levels of achievements, every successful life needs active positive forces operating in it. It takes strong, deep-rooted, positive forces in a person's life to ignore wind-bending negative obstacles. It takes committed, dependable positive forces in a person's life for him or her to maintain focus on that which is good. It takes knowing God personally and accepting Jesus Christ as the way to salvation.

Knowing God, through Jesus Christ is the most effective means by which negatives are turned positive. Through this spiritual relationship with God, a person life is equipped to face whatever challenges life presents. It is a faith walk that gives people the courage to trust God and to choose those life-giving qualities such as love and hope to apply passion to accomplish their dreams and goals.

Courage requires passion from people that want to move from being negative thinkers to people living their lives as positive dreamers and achievers. However, without passion people with low self-esteem often refuse to move their meaningful living opportunities from saturated negativism, and negative environments. Therefore, success-oriented people must have the courage to speak up and make it clear that they are willing to turn their life's challenges from negatives into positives.

I have come to understand that it takes both courage and passion in the life of goal-oriented people for them to become successful, even in the face of criticisms and discouragements. Therefore, when a person dares to reach out for greatness, he/she will not settle for the less. When a person dares to dream beyond his/her present condition, he/she will not bow down to failure. When a person dares to face the truth about his/her life, with all flaws and imperfections unveiled, he/she will not be shamed by what's revealed. For courage to have the strength and the ability to move people in positive passionate directions, they must be willing to examine two things about themselves: that which is in the heart and that which is in the mirror. The heart because that is where the true person lives, and the mirror because that is who the person sees.

The way a person thinks reveals what is in the person's heart, and what's in the heart speaks to his/her view of life. Therefore, if a person thinks that the world owes him/her something, then that person will more likely spend life in a valley of excuses, that is, blaming everyone except self for the way life is treating him/her. In this kind of person's attitude, life becomes boring, unfulfilling, and meaningless. People with this way of thinking are often found working for the paycheck that never satisfies. There is an urgent need for passion.

Positive changes occur when people dare to face the mirrors of their lives, and despite both perceived and recognized imperfections, they still like who they are, and what they see. Society and the world we live in are significantly strengthened when we reinforce the concept that life becomes a success story only when people dare to live, the willingness to work, and the passion to make it happen. Life holds unlimited possibilities when you have the will to live and the drive to succeed.

Happy are the people who choose pathways that lead them to the dream and the work they want to do for a lifetime. Liking what you do with your life is only one part of the process that brings fulfillment. The greater part is found in the personal spiritual relationship one has with God. I am talking about a passionate spiritual relationship. The kind of passion-filled with spiritual energy that produces good things, and at its best, it explodes into enthusiasm. Passion is that inner drive that motivates the human spirit to seek for the highest and to give the very best. There is a need for this passionate dynamite in people's hearts if they are to reach their spiritual destinies. The power to succeed on this spiritual journey is found in the life, love, and spiritual intimacy that each person has with God. When passion is the driving force in a person's life, coupled with the personal desire to live spiritually, success will breach all hindering barriers.

Doing what you like to do with passion is a calling from God. People seeking to build their dreams must include having a passion for success to make life discoveries lasting experiences. Life must be viewed as being too precious to live carelessly, aimlessly, or insignificantly. Equally, work must be seen as an opportunity to succeed. Work becomes a personal statement to the world of one's passion, drive, and willingness to contribute to building a better society. A lazy person does not share this testimony, nor understand the value and the worth that work offers all who participate in the process. Lazy people have been misled to believe that they can get satisfaction from just being alive and doing nothing; or by waiting for someone else to do for them; or by stealing what others have worked hard to gain. This is faulty thinking, for the Bible tells us in II Thessalonians 3:10b (KJV), "that if any would not work, neither should he eat."

It is written in the Bible that from the beginning it was purposed by God for man to work. The creation story in Genesis chapters one and two tells us that all that exists in the world was created by God for a purpose. God's plan and purpose for mankind (that was created just a little lower than the angels) was to care for the Garden of Eden and the created creatures. Man's purpose and role in the world were important in carrying out God's plan. God planned to create a world and put the man in charge of that world. To help man define his purpose in the world, God gave him detailed works to fill his day. God knew that an idle day would become an empty day. One of the first works assigned to Adam was giving names to all things created. Each day Adam was busy doing his work classifying and identifying every creature and thing God had created. However, God determined that it was not good for Adam to be alone.

Therefore, God created from Adam a companion that we know as Eve, but Adam called her "woman" because he said, "this is now bone of my bones, and flesh of my flesh: she shall be called woman because she was taken out of man," (Genesis 2:23, KJV). Together, these two were given the responsibility of tending to the Garden of Eden.

However, sin was introduced into the world when Adam and Eve disobeyed God. At that moment of disobedience, the world was changed from being a perfect environment to that of a flawed reflection of perfection it once was. Adam and Eve's disobedience of God cost them their perfection. Their spiritually perfect relationship with God had been forever changed. The spiritual fellowship they shared with God, because of sin, was not any longer the same. For their sake, Adam and Eve were put out of the Garden of Eden to live in a world they had to discover on their own. In this new world order pain became real, fatigue and tiredness were in the daily work, and living a full and expressive life would no longer be without cost. They had to work harder to live and survive. Because of sin, hard work was now part of the living world of Adam and Eve.

Work continues to be the essential process by which people build their dreams, and passionately pursue goals that motivate desires, in them, to achieve and become successful in life. Therefore, we must passionately embrace the power of work, and like the work that we do if we are to become successful in our world. Liking what you do with your life, your career, and your dream makes work a needed tool to reach, attain, and envision a successful future.

I have engaged this moment and seized this opportunity to discuss the importance of having passion, working passion. Whether you are working on a dream unfilled, an incomplete career move, or restoring and maintaining intimate relationships, or becoming more spiritually communed with God, passion is the key to working it out.

The primary focus of this writing is about passionate Love, having a passionate Life, and a passionate Intimacy with God. It is my prayer that all who read this definition of a passion-filled life will be inspired enough to take every opportunity to live superbly every day by doing what you like doing with passion.

CHAPTER 1
PASSIONATE LOVE

It was during the late 1980s that rhythm and blues singer Tina Turner returned to the top of the Billboard chart singing her number one hit, "what's love got to do with it?" The song, which was also the title of a movie made about the life and love relationship of Ike and Tina Turner, spoke of the hurt, pain, lack of faith and lack of confidence she had come to expect from this thing called love. Words in the song asked the question, "Who needs a heart when a heart can be broken?" This sad question references people that feel betrayed by love. Love is that cohesive warmth that the heart longs to feel, and yet, too often it becomes an insincere tool that yields heart-felt pains and brokenness. Love, by definition, is an expression of endearment. It is often sought as a precious confirmation of caring.

Passionate love is sometimes misrepresented by emotions and emotional feelings. The results of this kind of expression of misunderstanding love become clouds of emotional confusion. Valued love relationships that should be building blocks for a passionate living often end in broken marriages, divorces, and couples living together to avoid commitments. Live-in partnerships, and uncommitted dating are all signs and symptoms of a loss of trust and love in relationships. So, the question remains, "what's love got to do with it?"

According to the Bible, love has everything to do with how we live, how we care for each other, and how we relate to God. The truth of the matter is that we cannot honestly give real love or experience true love without God. It is written in I John 4:8, that God is love. God's love is real! It is an unconditional love that makes life meaningful and living a purposeful journey. It is a depth of love that calls men and women together in firm gripping relationships and holds them in loving embraces. It is the kind of love that is patient enough to allow the hearts of lovers to learn, at their own pace, how to meet the needs, wants, desires, and fulfillment of the one they love. True love is a journey filled with passion.

CHAPTER 2
TRUE LOVE VERSUS FALSE LOVE

True love is real, genuine, and can be trusted to gain roots in the heart of the one you love. However, false love is deceitful, destructive, and pretends to befriend the heart of the person, only to be exposed as a fraud. False love is self-seeking emotions that rob the heart of longevity and stability. All who believe its promises will be discarded, discouraged, and left with a lack of trust in love again. False love brings confusion by offering sweet things that turn sour; artificial flowers that will not bloom; and eternal promises that won't last past a day. False love does damage to the heart and leaves an emptiness in the souls of would-be believers in the promises of love. Life's journey would be a disaster if false love were all that the heart encountered. Fortunately for the seekers of lasting intimacy, true love is also available as life events push us forward past the disappointments.

True love can be recognized for what it is, a sweet fragrance of trust. Its smell is fresh and refreshing but not overbearing. It speaks in whispering sounds for easy embrace and romance of the heart. It is plain in appearances. There are no hidden facial expressions or dishonest emotions associated with it. True love reflects the God-kind of love that can be trusted. This great love is filled with passion, care, and concern for others. It is the strength that secures broken hearts and rebuilds bruised confidences. Love is about long-lasting relationships.

The relationship between a man and a woman is a God-ordained partnership designed to guide them on a journey toward life, love, and completion. The love shared between a man and woman is precious in the sight of God. That is why love must be passionately pursued, captured, and stored in the heart. It cannot be used as a game played between the sexes or saved by locking it in a box. Love must be free to connect heart to heart. It must be strong enough to endure times of fleshly wanderings and weaknesses. Love must be a mending instrument by which the heart is filled with joy and happiness. Therefore, true love shared between man and woman has the power and magnetism to draw two lives together, shape them, and make them one. Adam and Eve were the first to share this experience.

CHAPTER 3
DOING MARRIAGE WITH PASSION

Marriage is the first institution ordained by God for the purpose to establish and maintain a love relationship between man and woman. The Bible states in Genesis 2:24, "therefore, shall a man leave his father and mother, and cleave unto his wife: and they shall be one flesh," (KJV). From that time and throughout human history marriage has been heralded as the consummation of a love relationship. However, in recent years, marriage has not been the ultimate act of relationships. For many, marriage represents bondage and a restriction they do not want to be attached to. Therefore, they choose to share unbinding relationships, such as living together, and partial house-sharing. This type of living permits them to leave whenever, without feeling obligated to the person of the sanctity of marriage.

This flawed perception of marriage has eroded the hope and long expectation some may have had entering into this sacred union, by offering them the concept of trying to see if it works, rather than being committed to making marriage work. Marriage, as I have come to understand and observe, is not a finished product that couples enter into at a wedding ceremony. Rather, it is a process of growing, knowing, and coming together to build a life that brings the two into the union of being one home, family, and love. There are four areas of focused interest that successful marriages are based on: communication, finances, sex and intimacy, and the engagements of family and friends. The roles these topics play in a marriage usually determine the success or failure of marriage relationships.

COMMUNICATION (Let's Talk About It)

Communication is the foundational key to the success

of any organization or relationship, but none more significant than in a marriage relationship. In my years of counseling couples preparing for marriage I have greatly emphasized, to the highest degree of relevance, the importance of good, clear, understandable communication between them. Without good communication couples often end up unhappy, bitter, hateful, and divorced. A lot of reasons are attached to such dreadful endings with the correct reason, lack of communication, never acknowledged. Talking is often confused with communication. When couples are asked, did you talk about it? Could you talk about it? Were you willing to talk about it? The answers are almost clichés, "we talk all the time." The problem here is, talking is not equal to communication. The differences between the two are, talking is words, communication is understanding. Couples assume that because they have known each other for long periods or have been around each other for a while, they share the same language or definition of language. I have learned and observed that different families have different ways of talking to and communicating with each other, and whereas we may say or hear the same word or words, the meanings and expressions usually are aligned with how families have interpreted them. Therefore, couples joining their lives together need to spend time not only sharing words, but also the meaning of the words. In my counseling I use a common word, such as "BARK," and I ask the couple to respond to the word without thinking about the word and give the first thing that comes to mind. Sometimes couples say the same words, other times they differ. "Bark" could be the sound of a dog, a part of a tree, or a person shouting at you. When the couple agrees on the same definition, they are on the road to communicating with each other. The more words shared the better the relationship becomes. Communication is a key element to marriage success.

FINANCES (Show Me the Money)

Another key element in the process of successful marriage relationships is financial management, control, and distribution. It is quite common for couples "in love" to overlook all the aspects required to keep love in their relationship. Money is a needed and required source for living. When couples come together in relationships they must talk about their financial incomes, debts, obligations, schedule of payments, as well as their savings and checking accounts. Then they should communicate, with each other, as to how they will allow money in their relationships to be assets and not liabilities. Therefore, communication is essential. When it comes to financial management there is not a one-size-fits-all format. Each family, household, or couple has to determine how they will efficiently manage their financial resources and family needs. Money can help build a marriage, or it can cause it to implode. It helps when couples communicate, work together, and plan how to apply it to their shared goals. Money becomes a destructive force when couples fail to talk about and communicate their money issues and concerns. When secret accounts or undiscussed spending become active roles in the marriage relationship, the result usually ends up being the erosion of trust, lack of accountability, and destroyed marriages. To avoid allowing money to become a hindrance to the love you share or interfere with the married life you are building together, couples must not hide their monetary resources from each other. Neither should cheat physically or monetarily; nor misrepresent their monetary value or worth.

Just show me the money!

SEX AND INTIMACY (What's Love Got to Do with It?)

It is a misnomer to speak of love and sex as being the same expression of endearment and commitment. Because when the two are not properly engaged and applied, the marriage relationship often suffers. Many couples begin their marriages under the allusion that sex will keep them together only to discover that sex alone will not satisfy their marital longings, demands, and requirements. At the beginning of the relationship, the passionate drive for sex is fulfilled in sexual desires and sexual activities. However, after a few months of sexual bliss, many couples discover that sex alone is not enough to keep the relationship exciting, motivating, and desirous. Sex alone will not keep marriages from failing. Therefore, intimacy must partner together with sex to ensure that marriages will develop in relationships. Sex and intimacy's involvement will enable couples to maintain interest in each other, provide the energy to sensuously perform, and give them the longing desires, commitment, and efforts to bring pleasure to their partner, the one that is loved. Intimacy, to please and bring pleasure to the one you love, is expressed in various ways to show how much you care. Such actions may include giving flowers, sharing candlelight dinners, setting the mood for quiet moments of ecstasy, leaving a tender love note, and/or a timely phone call that says, "I love you." This question, what's love got to do with it? continue to pursue couples determined to make their marriage a success. The answer to this question, for such couples, is found in the loving relationship they share, and their marriage that is explored in sex and defined through intimacy.

<u>FAMILY AND FRIENDS</u> (It's A Family Affair)

The role that family and friends play in marriage relationships can be either a strength or hindrance to the success of the married life being built. Family and friends must be thought of as support to the marriage, but not to be too involved in the relationship that their participation may cause a schism, or a negative environment for the couple in the marriage. Family and friends need to be encouraging reminders to couple to value their lives together, and that their relationship should contain laughter, doing fun things, keeping sacred things sacred, and never forgetting where they've come from. Family and friends must be a strength to help build this marriage. It is a family affair.

CHAPTER 4
PASSIONATE LOVE RELATIONSHIPS

The love relationship between Jacob and Rachel is a story that's filled with passion, devotion, and sacrifice. Jacob and Rachel met one day at the community well where all the animals watered. Jacob had come to this place from his distant homeland escaping the wrath of his twin brother Esau that he had angered by stealing from him his birthrights as being the oldest son. Jacob helped Rachel water her father's sheep and learned that she was the youngest daughter of his uncle Laban, his mother Rebekah's brother, of whom he was seeking to find a place to live. Jacob was in awe of Rachel from the moment they met and asked permission to marry her. With having little to no personal resources of his own, Jacob asked permission to work as compensation to marry Rachel. His uncle Laban, being a trickster and deceiver as Jacob had been, committed Jacob to work seven years to attain the right to marry Rachel. According to Jacob (Genesis 29:20), those seven years seemed like but a few days because of the love he had for Rachel. Jacob loved Rachel and this was evident on the morning after he was supposed to have married her. After the seven years were completed, a great wedding party was given for Jacob and his bride Rachel; or so he thought. When the morning came Jacob discovered that he had been deceived. He had not married Rachel, whom he loved, but rather her older sister Leah. He was upset by what had occurred and confronted his uncle for not honoring their agreement. His uncle Laban explained the custom they practiced, the younger cannot be married before the older. Not to be outdone, because he loved Rachel, he agreed to work an additional seven years to have her as his wife. His uncle agreed because God was blessing Jacob in everything that he was doing, and therefore Laban was being blessed as well. The love Jacob had for Rachel was genuine. It was passionate to the level that time required to have her was a small sacrifice. To this love union, two sons were born that they named Joseph and Benjamin.

CHAPTER 5
"I LOVE MY HUSBAND"

One day a few years ago, while working as a sales clerk at Gospel Supply House, a Christian bookstore, I was talking to a woman who was buying a valentine gift for her husband. I noticed a certain glow about her, and I asked her what was it that she was trying to find. She explained that she was shopping for something special for her husband. She was excited because it was a special day to express their love for each other. Looking at her being so happy, I assumed that this woman, who looked to be in her forties, was a divorcee whose life had been rekindled by a new marriage, or a new relationship, or a new life interest. Without further speculation, I asked her how long she and her husband had been married. Her answer was surprising, "Thirty years, and I am so happy." I was shocked at such a strong positive response to a question about marriage. Not that old-fashioned thing called marriage, I thought! We live in a time where marriage is an outdated exercise in companionship. Because of the free expression of love movement, many people have concluded that marriage is a burden they choose not to carry around with them. In this no-commitment love zone many have adopted the mindset, live with whom you like, as long as you like them, and when you stop liking them, move out. No strings attached. No property to decide. It is everyone for self.

It was like a glass of cool lemonade on a hot summer day when I heard her say, "I love my husband." You do what? Is not love something you say when you are trying to manipulate something out of someone? Is not love just a byword you say to keep peace in the house? What about that fake kiss given every morning to fool your partner into thinking that you are still in love? This is a new age! What's love got to do with anything? Yet this dear woman without shame, regrets, or apologies smiled and spoke of her love, marriage, and romance as though she was a newlywed awaiting her honeymoon. Isn't that great? Isn't that wonderful? Isn't this a great sign that all is not lost? Isn't it good to know that true passionate love is like a deep-rooted anchor that is lowered into the depths of the heart? Yes, it is good to know that true love will securely hold you through the years.

Years have passed since that shopping day occurred. I will always remember this dear lady and the joy she expressed as she spoke of loving her husband. It was easy, from her expressions, for everyone to tell how important her husband was to her. Her every word built him up. She described him as someone deep in her heart. There was passion in every word. Passion was in her search for the gift of love she was giving to her beloved. Passion was in the pride she displayed for the marriage and love relationship she and her husband shared. It was easy to believe that passion was in the vows they made before God on their wedding day to love each other forever. I did not know for sure about their wedding day, but I knew that passion was in all that she was doing to make this day, a reminder of their great love.

Now and then I see this loving couple, either out in the community or at a church event and each time I do I find them showing that same kind of affection toward each other. When I see them together, they are either holding hands or sharing a smile. All can tell that they love being around each other. They love being with each other. They love each other. This happily married woman is named Mary Louise and the husband she loves is named Willie. In a time when relationships are individually defined, it is wonderful to find a relationship that is God-defined.

Mary Louise and Willie! Willie and Mary Louise! This loving couple is a wonderful model for romance. Their love has kept them true to their commitment, their vows, and the God they serve. As active church members, they serve faithfully in various capacities working side by side, hand in hand, and heart to heart. It is their love for each other that shines so bright. It is their love for each other that binds their hearts together. It is the refreshing and enduring love relationship of Mary Louise and Willie that is worth noting the passion they share loving one another.

CHAPTER 6
THE QUIET STREAM

Peter and Gloria met one day beside the quiet stream and fell in love. They had been victims of scorned and rejected love relationships. Although they were strangers searching for completion, their time together at the quiet stream caused them to become partners in a shared love relationship. Their previous deceptive love relationships left them unsure about their ability to trust this thing called love. They came to the quiet stream seeking what they desperately needed, confirmation of true love. While considering the aspects of their roles in the failed love relationships, their thoughts were immersed in dark clouds of uncertainty. They wondered whether their failed love relationships were the results of them allowing their lives to become too routine, predictable, or dull to maintain the love interest of their partners. Not knowing the true answers, they sought what they needed most, to be loved. They needed relationships that made them feel important and loved.

The quiet stream, by legend, was a designated place of hope. Often people with life-defeating issues and problems would come to the stream seeking answers. Many have come before, and in the quietness of the stream, walked away with enriched enthusiasm, and the passion for living that gave new meanings to their lives, love, and relationships. The quiet stream's legend had the spiritual distinction of being compared to the Bible's pool of Bethesda found in the fifth chapter of the Gospel of John. Just as this pool's healing power rewarded the first person that was able to get into the waters after been stirred up by the Angel of the Lord of whatever health conditions they had, so could the quiet stream provide spiritual restoration.

Couples in love relationships often overlook the importance of the need for spiritual incorporation in the process of bonding with each other. The deception of feelings and emotions couples embrace believing that relational fulfillment can be attained through the physical without the need of the spiritual cause them to abandon their vows of commitment to each other. Peter and Gloria found themselves on common grounds having invested their love in physical confirmation at the expense of spiritually balancing the love in their hearts. Now, they are here at the quiet stream looking for the missing elements in their lives. Standing at the quiet stream seeking the kind of love that would be like, for them, a fresh breeze of wind encircling the quiet streams of their hearts.

Peter and Gloria had been looking for love in all the wrong places. They were searching for someone to care for them and bring excitement back into their lives. Their previous partners had given them empty, boring, and unfulfilled relationships that made intimacy and passion forsaken pursuits. With only hurt, pain, and reduced self-esteem they stood silently at the quiet stream. It was like therapy for their broken lives. However, when they discovered one another standing at the quiet stream, something happened. Without speaking a word to each other, they recognized a special connection within them. Things changed. Healing was taking place. The burdens, hurts, and pains that brought them to the quiet stream no longer had any power over them. They smiled at each other and felt happy. The quiet stream made the difference. They fell in love.

Although being at the quiet stream had given them a new perspective, there were still concerns and issues they each had to face. Peter came to the stream searching for confidence. Gloria had a negative view of herself. Peter was a quiet man who dreamed of greatness, had the skills and talents to become great, but lack confidence in himself to make his dream come true. Gloria was a beautiful woman with a body that often gained her compliments, but due to abuse, never accepted compliments to be genuine or honest. Peter had done well with his life. He had a good job, a great reputation for kindness in the community, and a great manager of his resources. Yet none of that filled the emptiness the lost love caused. Gloria was a highly skilled person that used her abilities to help others. She always made time to do good deeds for others. Yet she doubted whether others valued or cared for her as a person. She wanted to matter as a person. Not for her body, not for her deeds, but for being a person that mattered to someone. She needed a friend to help her overcome the negatives. The quiet stream appealed to Peter. Gloria was attracted to the image of herself at the quiet stream. At the quiet stream, Peter and Gloria's lives connected. They were able to replace negatives with positives, disappointments with hope, and rejected love relationships with a new alluring positive relationship. After making their confessions at the quiet stream, they joined hands with one another and committed themselves to a new and trusting love relationship.

Peter and Gloria stood together, and perhaps for the first time in their lives, they felt alive, loved, and completely happy. Their love became a romance. Peter expressed his love for Gloria in a poem entitled, "Good Morning Rose Petals."

Did I ever tell you how wonderful it felt?
To fall in love with you? How refreshing it was for me!

It was like a new day with a greater purpose.

You became a Rose waiting to blossom in my heart.

From the moment I came to know you,

A stream began to flow through my heart.

It revived my desire to love, and focused my attention

On the kind of love that will never leave me.

You are beautiful. It is a plain truth to see!

Yet your greater beauty comes from within you, and

It is felt in all that you do; in all that you say!

Like a blossoming Rose you are

A sweet fragrance of love that fills my heart.

Years ago, we wrote letters. We were nothing more

Than paper lovers. We dreamed of being together,

Being complete and being fulfilled.

I didn't know much about you, but I dreamed about you.

I imagined how I would respond when I saw you.

I had it all down in my mind, but things changed

When I looked for the first time into your lovely face.

I saw in you a perfect dream come true.

I could not help but appreciate what I saw in you:

A beautiful creation of God's handiwork. Because your

Love is real, and your words genuine, you are a Rose

Blooming in my life.

I am thankful for you being

By my side. Because now

I greet each morning with a Rose

In my heart and rose petals under my feet.

PART II

CHAPTER 7
LIFE PURSUITS AND SPIRITUAL PASSION

Recently, I attended a funeral service of a person I did not know. I was there in support of the family and to provide spiritual comfort to one of my church friends who was part of this family. I do not recall what caused the person to die, nor did it influence my presence to be at the service. It was important for me to be there for my church friend. Nevertheless, this funeral, like most, was an opportunity for the community of friends, neighbors, and well-wishers to come together and provide spiritual songs, prayers, and praises that would encourage this family in their time of grief and loss.

Funeral services, by their nature, are sad refrains. Even when deliberate efforts are made to liven them up, they remain to be ceremonies for the dead. However, some of the greatest acts of kindness people can do to help families during times of grief is to let them know that they are not alone, show them sympathy and empathy for their loss, and always leave them loving and caring words of expressions. Although the obituary gave me brief information about the person, it didn't reveal enough about the person's life for me to get a thorough appreciation of the life lived. Therefore, it caused me to wonder about the impact that living makes on those we know and encounter. It caused me to visualize life in the image of a portrait being painted as a process between birth and death.

The program did not hold a long narrative about the deceased person. It did not tell the unknowing audience much about the person's life. It had a birth date and a death date with the period between the two highlighting a few facts about the person. It told us that the person joined the church at an early age and continued serving until the end of life for that person. Being a faithful and dependent employee had worked more than 20-years at the same place of employment. That was all that is said about the person's life. However, there was a special section that listed names and associated relationships of grieving family members to the deceased.

Therefore, I was left wondering about the part of the deceased person's life that was missing or not told. What were the missing details? What did the obituary fail to share with us about the deceased? What kind of life did this person live? Was the person introverted or extroverted? Did the person have a prominent social position? Or was this life wasted on a dream unpursued? What issues or conditions made this person cry? What did laughter sound like? What about having compassion for others? Or was selfishness everything? Did this person welcome each day with joy and enthusiasm or was each day another day of regrets?

Now in fairness to this funeral setting and/or other funerals, no one should ever read any obituary with the expectation that all these questions will or should be answered. The bigger issue is not about the questions, but rather the life of this person and every person. A person's life should be viewed as a journey traveled, a story told, and a monument on which meanings and purpose are built. Life is a precious expression of identity, and it should be lived with the passion of getting the most out of each day.

Building a great life can be compared to building a great wall or a beautiful house. It requires vision, sacrifice, and commitment. Vision gives life the spiritual insight to see the process toward the finished product. It is an image of personal development in the areas of self-appreciation, self-confidence, and self-expectation. Vision is a motivation to make dreams a reality.

Sacrifice is a required discipline in one's life if goals and dreams are to be reached. In building a life worth living, there are some things that one must forego, resist, and avoid. These things include wasting time, poor planning, lustful distractions, and apathy. Sacrifices to achieve the desired goals and dreams demand the willingness to give up the immediate pleasures for lasting satisfaction. Sacrifices require commitment.

Commitment is the purpose sealant that forms the kind of life that produces success. For people with dreams, and the passion to make them real, the goal in life is to succeed. The way to do this is to discard that which hinders and invest with loving passion all the elements that success requires. It takes work to get it done. Determined work! And

Committed work! Commitment won't let you quit, even when failures try to destroy your zeal to succeed. Commitment will not listen or give an audience to defeating voices, or discouraging situations. Commitment refuses to accept any shortcuts to successfully reaching the designated goal. Commitment combined with passion and hard work is only one way to properly succeed.

Life's fulfillment is achieved when a person chooses a career that is absorbed in the kind of passion for what he is doing and where that work becomes a pleasure rather than a task. Meaning has no meaning in a person's life if it lacks the passion that makes choice-making purposeful and meaningful. Choices, such as the career-work you will spend a lifetime doing; or living in ways that reflects your values and standards; or simply spending life doing whatever you like doing.

CHAPTER 8
SPIRITUAL PASSION FOR GOD'S PLAN

The spiritual passion needed in every person's life is based on knowing that God has a plan for your life. This spiritual plan, through your willing passionate pursue of your dreams, goals, and aspirations, will bring completion to your life. This spiritually passionate plan outlines the pathway to successfully achieving dreams and goals that are based on your interests, talents, and abilities. God's plan for you can be perceived as destiny or a divine calling that gives spiritual and passionate purpose to your life. God's plan is time-based. His time is not our time. Contrastingly, in our time, we construct the same personal growth and development timeline, as though everyone is the same. However, in God's time, His plan patiently develops each person individually, as he/she grows spiritually. In our time, we are often too impatient with each other and quickly give up on those that do not meet our expectations and/or requirements. But, in God's plan, He timely preserves the rejected, the overlooked, and the abandoned by planting in each person a restoring hope that pursues dreams and goals. Therefore, the question is not whether God has a plan for you, but rather, do you have plans that include God?

God's life plan is a work-centered passion that provides each person working satisfaction of growing and producing a fulfilled spiritual life. For those seeking purpose and passion in their lives, God's life plan is a rewarded challenging opportunity for success. That is if the person is willing to accept God's plan, work it through to achieve the desired dream or goal. However, those who fail to invest in God's plan for their lives are usually people who avoid the aspects of work; choosing rather not to seek opportunities to succeed or achieve anything beyond a day's pay.

There are social systems in our country that, by their designs, are established to encourage progress, and motivate people to invest in their future through work and personal achievement. However, the application and execution of such programs as the welfare system, employment services, and retirement programs have gone bad in its practice, and instead of providing upward mobility often stifled such positive results for poor people in general, and people of color specifically.

The welfare system, in the beginning, was established as an opportunity for families struggling through difficult times and financial hardships to receive temporary assistance, but like all bureaucracies, the welfare system took on a life of its own. Instead of it remaining an avenue by which people could get a hand-up on their way to reaching their dreams, it became a dead-end street, restricting participants to dependent handouts. Although the welfare system does some good, as a whole, it works against those it is supposed to help by preventing people from working their way out of this dependence and penalizing those that try to escape its control. For example, if a person gains any income beyond the amount given to them by the welfare system, it is taken away from them by reducing the amount given in the monthly check. Therefore, they are kept at the same monetary levels. The system stifles initiatives and hinders desires to excel. The good is lost because the system discourages work, and work, for humans, is the passion of life.

Retirement is the other seed that is sown against the wholesome efforts of work. Retirement should be the reward of hard-worn, passionately given, and ultimately committed workers in a work that has exhausted its tenure, and earned its time of rest. However, this rest should not be addressed as a time of lounging, doing nothing, and wasting away. Although retirement suggests the end of working and concludes that there is nothing else to do with your life. This mindset must be rejected. Retirement should not be on the minds of working people. Work should be your motivation to show up at the job each day. When people in the workplace spend their quality work time thinking about retirement they fail to enjoy the work they are doing. Workers focused on retirement will reduce their productivity, and cause them to devalued an appreciation for the work they do. It will also expose their lack of passion that motivates their work to good results. Instead, such distractions will yield, with such workers, bad attitudes, and job resentments because retirement is their desired goal.

Passionate workers possess the God-kind of quality

elements within their mind, heart, and spirit that enable them to perform their tasks at high levels. These are the kinds of people that God is looking for to model the right attitude toward work that leads to retirement. These are people who can be trusted with important assignments; who will get the job done without resentments. Unfortunately, not every worker shows up at the job to do the work. Retirement takes people out of the game of life regardless of the gifts, skills, and talents they have that immensely contribute to the betterment of others. Retirement is a social ill that often still the progress that living a passionate life that work has produced. Retirement, in the life of spiritually-minded people, must be discarded as an agent of discouragement, and reorient its purpose as an opportunity to utilize the training, skills, and experiences gained to use for greater works that life presents to you.

CHAPTER 9
WORKING TO REBUILD A WALL

The nation of Israel had fallen under the captivity of the Persian government, and the Israelites had been stripped from their homeland and made slaves. The city of Jerusalem was ravished. The walls, which served as protector and security for the city, had been torn down. The defeat of Israel by the Persians was disheartening, but the demolition of the wall was a devastating blow to the spirit of the people who now felt abandoned and destroyed. It was after this awful ordeal that God needed a "take charge" worker who could lead other workers into completing a specific task assigned by God. The man who accepted the job was not one in a commanding position but was rather a wine taster and slave to Persian King Artaxerxes. His name was Nehemiah who could have considered himself as being in retirement. After all, he was just a wine taster. However, his love for Israel prompted him constantly think of Jerusalem, and inquire about its condition. One day he asked one of his fellow Jewish brothers who had escaped captivity, and who had recently come from Jerusalem, the condition of the city. The news he got was discouraging. He was told that the city was in distress, and the walls were torn down. Nehemiah knew that as long as the walls were down there could be no peace or safety in the city and among the people. What could he do about it? He was a slave in a strange land. However, the lesson that Nehemiah learned about trusting God, believing God, and honoring God by doing the work of God should inspire all of us, if we have not already been inspired, to sign up to work for God.

Nehemiah came before the king with a troubled heart, which could be seen by his actions and in his face; this was not a good thing because the king did not permit sad people or bad news to be in his presence. Nehemiah panicked when he was discovered. The king himself asked him what was wrong. If God had not been with him, if God had not accepted his resume of faith for work, if God had not planned to use him, he could have been in trouble; but God was with him, for him, and waiting to use him. Unknown to Nehemiah, God was at work in the heart of the king and caused him to not only permit Nehemiah to leave his wine-tasting job to rebuild the walls of Jerusalem but also provided him all the building resources and protection he needed to do the work. God wants workers who are willing to trust him. He will do the rest.

When Nehemiah got to the city, he found it in as bad a condition as it had been described. The spirit of the people that remained was low and they were afraid. They could have been working, but they were afraid of the people who did not want them to build. The plan that God gave Nehemiah to build the wall was not a one-man job. It required the involvement, cooperation, and participation of others. He needed willing workers who wanted to work, and who would take pride in doing God's work. Before any work could be done Nehemiah had to know and be aware of what needed to be done. Therefore, he walked around Jerusalem alone surveying the conditions of the city. Once he became aware of what it took to get the wall built, he took a second walk around the city with the Elders and leaders of the people. He wanted them to have the same picture of urgency that he had. The third thing he did was enlist the people's participation by getting their approval and involvement in getting the job done. He spoke to them about the condition of the wall, the city, the people, and of how Jerusalem city lay wasted, the gates burned with fire. He appealed to them to join him in building up the walls of Jerusalem so that God's people would no longer be subjected to defeat from their enemies. "Then I told them of the hand of God that was good on me. And they said, let us rise up and build, so they strengthened their hands for this good work," (Nehemiah 2:18, KJV).

It took them only 52 days to complete this enormous task because Nehemiah was a man who loved his work and working with him were others who took pride in doing what they did. Chapter three of the book of Nehemiah tells of men who side by side joined together their skills and talents to get the job done. Each person was given a specific area on which to work on restructuring the wall. Completion of the task of rebuilding the wall depended on everyone doing the specific task they were assigned. The work they were doing began with them sharing the vision of a rebuilt wall that would provide them peace and security. It required workers who wanted to do their jobs. The work was too important a task to give to anyone who did not want to be there or did not share the vision. Nehemiah knew that with vision, unity, and willing workers, he had the essential tools for success. The people went to work, each man to his task, and every task a man. The completion of the job required total focus and concentration because there were many distractions to deter their labor and discourage their spirits.

For Nehemiah, the distractions came from the voices of three men who did not want him to succeed in rebuilding the wall. These men tried to discourage him by pretending to be his friends, by making fun of what the Israelites were doing, and by showing false interests in the security of the Jewish people. Their names were Sanballat, Tobiah, and

Geshem. These men were angry with the Jews for rebuilding the walls, and they conspired against them to tear it down. They pretended to honor Nehemiah as the leader of the people and invited him to join them. They wanted him to stop working and spend his time talking with them. Nehemiah was a worker who would not be discouraged or distracted. His enemies sent for him again and again requesting him to take a break from his work assignment and come share time with them; as though they cared for him.

In chapter six and verse three he answers them with a simple response, "I am doing a good work, so I cannot come down." By "good work" he meant doing the Lord's work. Nehemiah's divine destiny was calling him forward, not backward, or sideways. Through his commitment to his assigned task, and because of his faithfulness to the work of God, he was allowed to engineer a recovery plan that had the wall rebuilt in a remarkable time of only 52 days. It is remarkable what will occur when work becomes life, and life is passionate works. When you are busy working, God will perform miracles right before your eyes. Nehemiah was a hard worker, a spiritual worker. He was one whose work ethic motivated him to pursue and achieve his spiritual destiny. What about you? Are you going to work? Or are you just hanging around the house!

Remember, when the alarm clock goes off it is time to get out of bed. You know that you have to, even if you do not want to, get up! You are in pursuit of your spiritual destiny. Adjust your mindset so that you are not greeting another miserable day. You are not going to a lousy job that you hate, but rather a passionate work that is a ladder that will elevate you to greater possibilities. You will not spend your day or your time with people that you cannot stand or tolerate, but rather you will develop networks, friendships, and partnerships. Going to work will become as natural as life itself. You will take pride in your work. You will enjoy the work you do.

CHAPTER 10
A WOMAN NAMED DEVON

The alarm clock goes off. It is time to get out of bed. You know it already, but you do not want to do so. The annoying sound of the alarm clock introduces you to another lousy day; one that will take you to a dead-end job that you hate; a job that will require you to work with people you either do not like, cannot stand, or both; but you reluctantly get up and participate in this miserable daily process. You have to live and you need the money.

As depressing as this scenario presents itself, it probably depicts many people who have lost the zeal of making work a personal act of pursuing lifetime dreams, and have allowed living to become an empty circle of shortcomings and regrets. However, when a person has the right attitude and the right motivation to work, every dream can become a reality. Every vision will provide the required energy that will build your life into that dream. It is rather uncommon in today's world to find people who genuinely love their work, take pride in their work, and are willing to work uncompromisingly until the work is done. As rare as this may be, I recently discovered such a person who has this kind of passion for the work that she does. She is a woman with a passionate attitude for doing her work and getting it done at the highest levels of excellence. She serves her community as the elected city clerk for a small Alabama town. She likes what she does, and she does her work joyfully and with a positive attitude. She is a down-to-earth person. She never overlooks or talks down to anyone because of her position. She treats people the way she wants to be treated. She is both positive and energetic in doing her job. Her name is DeVon! She is passionately motivated by the principle of wanting to do the job right the first time and every time. DeVon's motivation to do her work at such a highly proficient level of output began with a dream she had years ago for serving her country through the military. For her, going to the military was a natural progression in the legacy of her family's tradition. Although several family members had military careers before her, DeVon viewed the military as a patriotic duty and a call to serve the country she loves.

DeVon was all prepared to enter the U.S. Air Force when an early pregnancy interrupted that dream. For her, serving in the military was a high calling, an opportunity to protect the ones she loves. She saw her role in the Air Force as being part of a "blanket of security" for America and protecting family members all across the country, but it did not happen. Disappointed and hurt that this dream could not be fulfilled, she moved forward with her life. Although she had a great love for the Air Force, she did not regret the reason why she would not serve in the military. Instead of sitting around thinking about what did not work, DeVon refocused her aim and headed off to college. She pursued and earned a degree in computer technology. She devoted her life to working for her family and serving the public.

I was amazed and inspired as I listened to her talk about how much she loved her work. She was focused. She was excited. She was eager to share details of her routinely busy days at work. During our discussion, I did not hear from her any negative words or complaints about the workload, or anything else to suggest that she was not happy doing what she likes to do. I learned that in performing her job at such high levels of excellence there would be days when she had to work late hours or come in to do early hours, but neither deterred her attitude or her focus because she knew the importance of getting the job done.

Such a person with this positive way of thinking and committed attitude is a gift and a blessing to the workplace and the people she serves. This commitment to her office caused DeVon to wake up each day focused on the work that demands flawless execution of the numerous tasks assigned to her. Immersed in her tasks, DeVon finds satisfaction from her work performance knowing that at her best she has served the public well. For her superb work performance, positive attitude, overall commitment, DeVon is highly regarded as an expert and a valuable team member by people in the law enforcement field. In addition to the law enforcement people, she is also greatly respected by the people that come to her office and she helps each day. You can tell by her actions that she finds joy in doing her work.

Her warm personality makes it easy for folks to talk to her. Most people that meet her are glad to know her. That is exactly the way it was for me when I came to know her and spent time with her.

I will forever treasure the first day that I knowingly walked into her presence. It was a spiritual impact moment for me. It touched my heart. As I recall, when I first saw her, Devon was deeply immersed in her work in the courthouse. I stood there looking at her waiting for her to notice me. She was not distracted by my presence. She continued doing her work until she had a break before she looked up and acknowledged my presence. The first moments we shared were brief, but meaningful, precious, and ones I will treasure forever in my heart. I did not realize it as much then as I do now, but God used the reason I was in the city to bring our lives together. Being unaware of any connections with her, I was made aware that this great professional, passionate working woman was my sister. We share the same biological father but have different mothers. Because we did not grow up together nor around one another, we knew very little about each other. I remember seeing her when she was a little girl around the age of five or six, but as time passed, we did not maintain active relationships.

On that first day of reacquaintance, her mother who was so kind and loving toward me told me that my sister worked at the courthouse. I was anxious to see her and reintroduce myself to her. When I visited her job, she was working busily with her task. When I introduced myself to her, she expressed both surprise and excitement. Her first words to me were filled with joy. She recognized me! That was a happy moment for me; a really special moment for me that I will keep. From that day forward there has been nothing but happiness between us. As I have come to know her, I am inspired by her enthusiasm, her work ethic, and her love for what she does. I am proud of how she has taken charge of her life and made it a positive example. When her dream was deferred and she focused on her family and raising her children she did not lose sight of being a professional and passionately pursued working at high levels of excellence in her profession.

DeVon has a deep devotion to her family. She and her husband Steve share a genuine love for each other that extends back to when they were teenagers. They, like most couples, struggled early in their marriage relationship to make things work and stay together. She acknowledged that it was the love commitment that they made to each other that caused them to get through the tough times and find success in their relationship. A testament of their enduring love is noted in her observation, "from where we've come from to where we are, I never thought that we would have made it." They made it and raised two exceptional children, a boy, and a girl. DeVon said one of the reasons she has been so committed to her work, in addition to liking the work she does, is that she did not want to raise her children in the projects (public housing). DeVon said, "I truly love my children. I am at my best being a mama!"

The passion she injects into her work has earned her the confidence, admiration, and appreciation of those for whom she works, and those she serves. Now before you think that I am painting an unbelievable story about this woman named DeVon because she is my sister, I want to put that idea to rest. DeVon is a quality person all on her own. I am touched and inspired by her gentle spirit that welcomed me into her life. I am happy to share her love.

The word passion seems a natural description of DeVon's spirit, attitude, and willingness to succeed. Above her many positions and platitudes, DeVon is praised for being a genuinely real person. She is not perceived, by any, to be a phony person or a pretender. She is a real person that can be trusted and is well-liked by many. All you have to do is meet her, and you will know it for yourself.

As you know, many people work in public service careers, some liking what they do, and others do not. However, there are far too many of these public service workers spending their days complaining about life and the work they do, rather than choosing to do something else that would bring fulfillment to their lives. Truth be known, lacking the courage to make changes, these impassionate workers settle for complaining. What I find refreshing and infectious about DeVon is the courage she displays in finding joy and passion in the work she does.

What is behind this woman named DeVon that gives her such a warm persona? I learned that she credits her positive approach to work and life to her relationship with God. She said that she grew up in the church with a basic understanding of God, but it was not until very early in her adult life that she and God formed a personal relationship that changed her life.

In this spiritual relationship, she wants God to live in her and to guide her life. Through this spiritual relationship, she has learned the value of being a woman of God by reflecting God's love in everything she does, including working with people, speaking with people, and serving people. As a woman of God, she grew to understand that it was her spiritual calling and part of her divine destiny to love her husband and to encourage him to become the kind of man God expects of him. As a mother, she knew that it was important for her children to see her life as a spiritual example of righteousness. It was important to her for them to see Christ in her.

DeVon's passion and efficiency extend beyond her daily profession into her community involvement, family activities, and her love for and commitment to the church. She is not ashamed to be identified as a servant of God. Her faith in God matters to her. Therefore, the zeal that wakes her up each morning and takes her to her daily work is the same zeal she applies to work in the church; giving herself unselfishly to the spiritual growth and development of the church. God has used her passion to inspire other church members to give themselves unselfishly to the work of Christ. Encouraged by her husband Steve, she has learned to wait on God, watch Him work things out, and trust Him for the spiritual development of His church. With Steve as her partner, this woman named DeVon is a committed worker at her church. She is involved in a myriad of activities and responsibilities. She cooks, teaches children's Sunday school and Vacation Bible School. She serves as the assistant counselor for the youth department. She is also the church's financial secretary. When she was asked how she gets all these things done, she said, "I couldn't do it on my own. It is God who allows me to do it all." With her positive and professional attitude, coupled with her deep love and passion for all that she does, DeVon is destined to touch many lives and spiritually influence many people to pursue an attitude of excellence.

CHAPTER 11
DEBORAH, A WOMAN OF GREAT DEDICATION

In the great history of the Jewish people, there have been many leaders and many levels of leadership. There was the period of the patriarch (2348-1706 B.C.), where the people were led by family rule and family loyalty (Abraham, Isaac, and Jacob), which eventually became tribal leadership. The twelve tribes of Israel organized the family in a way that every citizen of the nation was not only accounted for but properties were claimed and recognized the same way. The priests represented the spiritual leadership throughout Israel's history. They served alongside all other leaderships over the people of God. They were the voices of God in keeping the laws of God. Aaron was designated the first priest to the people of God. He began this spiritual leadership as Moses' servant and his descendants became the tribe of Levi, which became known as the priestly tribe. They were given the responsibility of handling the sacred laws, keeping the temple, and enforcing the practices of those laws.

The prophets were the next group of spiritual leaders over God's people. These great men of God spoke to the world as the voice of God, the voice of authority. Their major function was to receive spiritual directives from God and speak to the people about the present and future events. They challenged the bad times with visions from God to assure the people to stay faithful to God because better days were yet to come. They warned the people during better days not to become settled or lose their spiritual focus, but rather continue to live for God and be prepared if and when difficult days and times come.

The next period of leaders was given to the kings (1095-587 B. C.) which was known at the time when kings sat on the throne ruling the people of God. During this time of leadership, there were both positive and negative kings that led the people of God. There were some good kings like Josiah and some bad kings like Jeroboam. There were some strong kings like David and weak kings like Ahab. There were some wise kings like Solomon who gave people life, and murderous kings like Zimri who took people's lives. Throughout this period more than forty kings exercised either positive or negative influences over God's people.

Then there was the period of the Judges (1394-1095 B. C.). During this time of leadership, there were fifteen Judges that led the people of God. Among the 14 male

Judges was one female Judge named Deborah, a prophetess, and the wife of Lapidoth, a man who supported his wife in obscurity. She became the one and only female Judge to reign over Israel. Deborah was known for her patriotism (Judges 4, 5). She was dedicated to her people and her position. God used her to bring victory to His people.

However, just as Deborah, the Judge in Bible history, was committed to her calling so is another Deborah, that I know and am acquainted with, who has dedicated her life to serving the community of special needs people. Before the world became politically correct these special needs people were generally called and labeled retarded. This Deborah, who for 47 years has been my wife and the love of my life, has encouraged me with her words and inspired me with her unselfish dedication to me and our family. Additionally, she has demonstrated a loving devotion, concern, and care for this special community of people that are often overlooked, ignored, or rejected.

Caring for the mentally challenged has drastically changed in recent years. The system of care changed from housing these patients, that are now referred to as clients, in primarily state-controlled institutions to having these clients live in communities as normal citizens of the society. This transition of care and lifestyle called for an adjustment by the managers or caretakers. Instead of treating these clients like mindless bodies that can be mishandled, abused, and not respected as people, they must now, and rightly so, be treated as people that have feelings, that hurt, and need to be handled with care; although, they may at times move or respond at a slower pace than some others.

Deborah's dedication to her work is significant because people doing her kind of work must be exceptional, patient, loving; yet stern, and determined to provide their clients all the assistance for normalcy as possible. This is not a work or job for someone who just wants to show up. This work requires passion to effectively perform its various tasks. The required commitment by those engaged in this kind of work must be embodied in a passionate attitude of service that helps men and women, often with a child-like mind, to live in an adult-oriented social environment. Working with the mentally challenged is a job that is unfulfilling for those lacking the passion to do such jobs, and are only looking for a paycheck. However, for those who care enough to passionately work with and for these very dependent human beings, the reward comes in seeing the brightness in their eyes, or the feelings of being appreciated. Deborah has the passion, care, and love for these disadvantaged clients that look to her for guidance and security.

It is my observation that if anyone was ever intended to work in this area of life it is my wife, Deborah. Each day she goes out to work with these clients with nothing but love for them in her heart. She cares about them, and she interacts with them in a way that they know they can trust her to have their best interests at heart. Many programs serve these clients, and through the years she's gotten to know most of these clients, from other programs, by name. She knows them and they know her and with enthusiasm greet her when she sees them out in public places. Deborah loves her work. She is passionately dedicated to her work, and she has joy in doing what she does.

It is her passion for the work she does that has promoted her through the years. Today she has a group home in a community that houses three clients. She is responsible for their care, living area, and social interaction twenty-four hours, seven days a week. It is her love, for family and God, that is the single highlight of her life and who she is as a person. All that she does is based on her love. When examined more closely, the love she shares comes from her relationship with God. Being a devout Christian, all her actions seem based on the church's teaching, "do to others what you would have others do to you." It is in her dedication that the passion of her work and labor of love can be seen, felt, and appreciated for these human beings who are counting on their caretakers to show them love, care, and respect.

CHAPTER 12
VISION FOR A CITY

Vision for a city is an urban relations ministry dream that has been in my heart for more than 27 years. It was a God-given concept planted in my mind and spirit but is yet to be shaped into reality. It is supposed to be a community-based ministry focusing on cleaning up run-down community living areas, revitalizing primarily the career hope of young adults who have become hopeless, have forgotten their dreams, and have given up the will to succeed. This God-given vision has a two-fold objective: people working with people to improve the community, and giving everyone in the community a purpose, worth, and meaning.

The plan for this urban relations ministry includes being housed in a building with essential office and training spaces large enough to serve the dream purposes. The office spaces will be used for administrative operations that perform tasks such as project planning, financial operations, and community outreach efforts. The training spaces will be used as teaching and skills development areas. The young adults and other interested persons can participate in this program, which is designed to give these future leaders, entrepreneurs, medical specialists, and community leaders, the discipline, training, incentives, and motivation to get back on track and pursue life goals that will achieve their dreams. Other basic skills for careers may be incorporated, such as barbering, cosmetology, food services, sewing, quilting, and other skills. Professionals and career skilled peoples will be recruited to support this community ministry as volunteers willing to give back and help others to rise and succeed in life. The training program will be structured as hands-on development by participants to equip them to qualify for long-term employments with community businesses, and other organizations.

In the beginning, I was extremely excited about this urban relations community dream because I perceived it as being a God-given directive. However, I soon discovered that a dream will remain an imagination until you have a plan to make it real. The problem I had in making the dream a reality was lacking the passion and commitment, and the inability to share the vision with others and make it plain enough that others would willingly join me in making it happen. Because the idea of the dream sounded good to me, I thought that others would be equally excited and willingly join me in making this dream a good work.

The most essential aspect of a vision is the ability to make it clear to the levels that participants will understand its meaning and become motivated by its purpose. It was

God who emphasized this importance when He instructed the prophet Habakkuk about the plans, He had for them. He told the prophet in Habakkuk 2:2, to first write the vision down, put it on paper, in physical forms, and make it in plain simple to grasp language. Second, let the urgency of vision capture their interest and concern to the degree that everyone that reads it will be motivated to run passionately to make its purpose the desired reality. However, because I did not make the vision plain, the enthusiasm for the dream lessened, in me, and ended up being wrapped in a list of excuses and reasons why it could not, and has not happened. Therefore, the vision of this urban relations community ministry has been dormant and incomplete during these idle years. The story could end here and it would be accurate as far as bringing the dream of "Vision for A City" to life.

CHAPTER 13
RICHARD AND VICKI (GOSPEL SUPPLY HOUSE)

Passion is a powerful driving force with the capable influence of motivating people to transform their dreams into life-achieving fulfillment. The passion that was lacking in my dream of establishing and developing an urban relations ministry was found in the life work of a wonderful Christian couple named Richard and Vicki Thomason who built a ministry around a Christian bookstore. For more than 30 years they were the efficient and spiritually effective owners of a business labeled, The Gospel Supply House.

The passion for their dream began very early in their relationship. Their faith in God enabled them to seek and trust God for their dream. Richard had become a Christian, and while working for a railroad company in Montgomery, Alabama, he spent many off-hours browsing and reading books in the Alabama Bible Society bookstore. Something about that store was a calling, he noticed, that sparked interest in him to pursue a bookstore of his own. The passion for this dream was further enhanced by the availability to purchase a local Christian bookstore in Tuscaloosa, Alabama called The Book Nook.

Richard and Vicki loved to shop and browse in the Christian bookstore. They also loved Christian books because the inspiration they received from reading these books made great impacts on their lives. However, the thought of owning and managing a bookstore of their own was always in the back of their minds. Therefore, one day Richard asked a dear friend to join him in prayer that he may know God's purpose and plan for him and Vicki concerning owning the bookstore. After several meetings, Richard's friend seemed to lose interest, but they later discovered that this friend had been making plans, that didn't include Richard and Vicki, to open his bookstore.

However, six months after the store opened, this friend decided that he was not in God's will and approached Richard and Vicki about buying the store from him. After much prayer, and what Richard and Vicki felt was a direct answer from God, they purchased the store from this friend. Over the next eight years, the store expanded three times in the location on 15th Street in Tuscaloosa, Alabama, before it moved to a site on McFarland Boulevard East in Tuscaloosa. At this location, Gospel Supply House remained an active, vital institute of ministry for the Christian community until it was sold to a well-established Christian bookstore chain in 2007.

Let me tell you, Gospel Supply House was more than a Christian bookstore to the community of shoppers who would come from far and near to share in and soak up the always cordial, friendly, and helpful spiritual atmosphere. Richard and Vicki's loving spirit and attitudes made it that way. It was an expression of their dream and the passion for ministry that made Gospel Supply House a special place to visit and shop. They understood the importance of treating people with the kindness they liked to be treated with themselves. Because of it, Gospel Supply House became known and respected as a place of ministry, and it was revered for the services it provided.

During these years of watching their dream unfold, success didn't change their spiritual focus, nor their devotion to God, neither their dedication to providing their customers the best service and quality products available. Richard and Vicki remained to be everyday people. Ministry, for them, was a personable work. People loved them because they were personable, sociable, and easy to know. Perhaps this is what made my time with them life-changing for me. Because of our relationship, and the spiritual warmth of knowing them, I will forever love, respect, and appreciate them for allowing me to find work in their dream, and the opportunity it gave me to find God's purpose and passion in what He would have me do.

The history of this spiritual bonding began a few years ago when I returned home from having served 10 years in the military. I was hired to work in their store. That's the way I initially looked at it, being hired to work in the store. My attitude, at first, about this job was without passion because, at this time, I did not see the value of working as a clerk in a bookstore. In the U.S. Army, from where I was coming home, I was a commissioned officer holding numerous leadership positions. I had people working for me, responding to my commands. Now, doing this kind of work was for me, in my thinking at that moment, was a step-down to humiliation, but I needed a job. It was difficult for me at first to feel good, or comfortably working in this bookstore, Christian or not. I could not, at that time, see the spiritual impact, and great spiritual education God was giving me that would later make a difference in my life.

I have been a Christian most of my life. Before I went into the U.S. Army, I was ordained as a preacher of the gospel and served as pastor of several local churches. After serving my country these years, I was coming home with the expectation of being selected as the pastor of my local home church. However, when I was not selected by this congregation, I was spiritually crushed. My morale was destroyed because I was so sure that God would have me at that church, doing the work of God. Discouraged and disappointed, I did not know what to do. The truth of the matter was I did not see the bigger picture of what God was developing in me. I had known the Thomasons from the time the bookstore was on 15th Street and each year while on vacation from the military, I would stop by Gospel Supply House to speak to them. Now that I was out of the military and Richard knowing that I needed something to do, he asked me to work for him. I agreed outwardly, but inside I could not see myself working in a bookstore. It just wasn't me doing this work. I thought. Nevertheless, I accepted the opportunity to have a job. However, just as I had told myself, it was not the job for me; I convinced myself that I was right.

I was hired to be a clerk. A sales clerk with the responsibility of helping customers find the appropriate gifts or items they needed. I was hired to be friendly and let the shoppers know that they were welcomed and appreciated as valued customers. It was my job to provide them the kind of service that would give them reasons to come again. There was nothing wrong with the job or the job requirements except that it did not fit me! I thought. I did not think it was right for me because I felt that I was better than this job. I deserved a higher position or title! I thought. I was just home from the military, and in the U.S. Army, I was somebody. I was a commissioned officer holding the rank of Captain. As a Captain, I had people under my command. I was a leader. People did what I said. As a former Captain, I felt embarrassed to be seen working in such a low position! I thought. Give me a mop and a bucket, there is no worst shame! I thought. What am I doing here? What about A Vision for A City? Why did I leave the military?

I have come to understand that on this spiritual journey God will teach us, develop us, and elevate us if we allow Him to work in us. This is what I learned in but a few short days of being at Gospel Supply House. Let me emphasize that my agony had nothing to do with any of the people that worked for Gospel Supply. They were all helpful, caring, and good people with whom I loved working with. Because of how I saw myself, I was my problem child. However, this attitude of mine changed one day when two elderly black women came into the store looking for some church materials. (Let me inject this point, I was the only black employee at this store, not counting the cleaning crew that came in the evenings). The salesperson assisting them did not understand what they were requesting because of broken speech, and culturally different wording of church ceremonial items and materials. As the other clerk was trying desperately lovingly to assist these wonderful customers, I noticed that frustrations were setting in on both sides. I offered my assistance. On the surface, this moment seemed a minor event in a day filled with activities, but for me, this time was an epiphany. My eyes were opened. This was my spiritual lesson. This is what I was learning. Positions do not make you big. Serving others is as high as you can go. God was reminding me of what He said to the apostles concerning judging people from the outside. In Matthew 23: 1-11 Jesus tells them to not seek positions for man's approval, but rather seek to serve; then they would be considered great. From this moment on, Gospel Supply was no longer a job for me, nor a place where I felt embarrassed to be seen. It was for me the place God would have me. A place where ministry was enhanced by the passion of the heart.

The Lord made known to me, in this Christian bookstore, what ministry was truly about. It is about touching the lives of people and making a difference for them. It was at Gospel Supply House that God rehabilitated my spirit by allowing me the joy of being involved in this daily ministry. When people came into the store, from that moment on, it became an opportunity for me to share Christ with them, not preaching to them, just serving them. There were days when customers would come into the store with wrong or negative attitudes, or chips on their shoulders, or feeling depressed and discouraged, or hurt and defeated, or some other ills. These people, these precious people, creations of God's love, needed something or someone to give them some hope, some inspiration, or some reason to expect something greater to happen to them or for them. God allowed me to be in the right position to share this ministry. This is what I would do. I would give them Jesus, not preaching to them, but by serving them in a loving spirit.

Through love and kindness, I wanted them to know that no problem they had was too big for God. It was my passion for God that gave me the courage and love to serve these people in need of the Master's touch. I had learned that valuable lesson at Gospel Supply House Christian bookstore watching Richard and Vicki's dream and ministry of love impact many people's lives.

Now I'm calling them Richard and Vicki on paper, but I have other names that I called them out of my respect for who they are. Richard is the kind of leader and person that titles are not that high on his list as long as you remember that he is the boss and you get the job done. When I began working at Gospel Supply most of the employees were married adults, and for the most part, everyone called each other by their first name. It was hard for me, having spent the recent ten years in the military to refer to the boss or leader by his first name. At the same time, I did not want to appear to be out of step with everyone else, so I merely started calling him what I would call any superior, "Sir." I was not doing it because I did not want to say his name. I wanted him to know of my respect. That I was not taking his friendship for granted or out of order. That I recognized and respected him for building this great ministry that was a blessing to all who came to shop (worship) there. "Sir" (Richard) is a man of God that I am thankful to have known all these years, to have worked for, and served with him. His passion for a Christian bookstore built an empire of love, friendship, and a great outreach fellowship.

His wonderful wife, Miss Vicki, is a woman of God with a beautiful spirit matched only by her love for God. Miss Vicki is the "First Lady" of Gospel Supply. It was and always will be her support of and encouraging words to her visionary husband that caused their dream to become reality. The First Lady is ever so gentle in her dealings with all people she encounters. She is a wonderful person, a loving mother (and now grandmother), and a devoted wife. It is their example and spiritual passion for what they do that serve as great reasons for anyone to trust God to bring to life whatever dream or vision that has been planted in the heart.

Gospel Supply House is gone now. The building, that once was a hallowed place for sacred shopping, now carries a new name. Nevertheless, the ministry Gospel Supply House provided and spiritually performed is a living testament that will be in the heart of the Christian community it served for years to come, and perhaps forever.

PART III

CHAPTER 14
THE CHURCH AND PASSION

Every Sunday morning all across this wonderful land called America, people of faith fill houses of God known as churches, to share their times of worship. In these services, prayers are lifted, choir members, in musical rhythm and sway, sing sacred and melodious songs of praise. Preachers/Pastors, both great and small, deliver prepared sermons designed to motivate their congregations to have greater faith in God. On this holy day of the week, people from all directions come to church, to God's sacred place of refuge, for the applied purpose of hearing words of hope, a message to confirm their faith and trust in God, and to find spiritual purposes for their lives. These God-seeking people come to worship the Lord out of genuine love for the church and deep respect for God. They do not come to church to barter or argue over who's in control of God's church. Nor do they come to worship the sacred with a religious agenda of their own. They just want to feel the presence of the Lord, to touch the "hem of His garment." They want to grow in faith and spiritual knowledge so that they will know how to trust God every day. It is this desire to know God that motivates them to come to worship each Sunday. However, many parishioners leave worship services, Sunday after Sunday, disappointed because the atmosphere for worship was missing. This prevented them from feeling the Spirit of the Lord and received their desired spiritual worship experience.

Worshipping God is what the heart of everyday people is motivated to seek. For these everyday Christians, the church is not a complicated place. It is not a political forum. It is not a religious or philosophical setting. It is not a playground for the insincere or the hypocrites. This is

God's house built for God's people to assemble, worship, and give thankful praises. These ordinary people believe that God's house is a place that offers hope, love, and healing. It is also a place that's opened to everyone who seeks freedom from the bondage of sin through faith in Jesus. It is a place where newborn people of faith are welcomed into the kingdom of God. It is a place where testimonies of the Saints are outreach voices to an unsaved society. In this place, the preached message of the church is a sacred invitation that allows hurting people to find comfort, sick people to get well, and lost people to be found through Jesus Christ.

Yet the reality for many worshippers in today's churches is that the preaching for many no longer captivates the hearts of the believers, and fails to attract the interest of unbelievers. The lack of spiritual growth and Christian development is one of several reasons for some members' changed attitudes and commitments towards the church. The Christian church has a great reputation and practice for reaching out to sinners by evangelizing the world for lost souls to bring them into the light of the church. However, the church has faltered greatly in maintaining many recruited members because these recent additions to the church's roll soon become disengaged with the many church events and activities that give them no spiritual meaning of church.

The lack of spiritual knowledge and understanding as to who or what the church represents impacts not only recruited members but others that have been in church all their lives. Church worship cannot change lives until those that call upon the name of the Lord have a clear understanding of their relationship with God, and His plan to further develop their faith. Christian members that base their relationship with God on their emotional enthusiasm for Him will experience limited spiritual growth. They will have what the Apostle Paul called in Romans 10:2 (KJV) "having a zeal of God, but not according to knowledge."

CHAPTER 15
SPIRITUAL LEADERSHIP

How does the church get back into the ministry of changing lives, giving hope to the despaired, and encouraging believers to live by faith? The answer to this question is found in the roles of pastors, preachers, and qualified teachers that have been given the biblical mandates, duties, and responsibilities of caring for and leading church people in their spiritual walks with God. The depth of spiritual leadership in a church will determine the preparation and readiness its members have to faithfully engage in this spiritual warfare. This spiritual leadership will determine how effectively members can stand against the wiles of the devil who "comes to steal, kill, and destroy" (John10:10). The pastor, being called to his position by God, has been given the primary spiritual mandate to shepherd the flock of God through expository teaching, preaching, and setting the right spiritual examples for living. God gave pastors authority to put things in order while holding them responsible and accountable for providing spiritual leadership to grow the peoples' faith.

The image of being a pastor may not always comport with the life of a spiritual leader. Distortedly, for some preachers and congregants, the image of being a pastor is often based on looks, the clothes he wears, the car he drives, the titles he holds, and unfortunately, at times, the type of showman he can be and perform. A pastor, by title, can be applied to any person identified and established through religious organizations and recognized by their religious governance to perform rituals, ceremonies, and activities. However, the Bible defines the position of pastors quite differently from religious organizations and deems them more significant. Pastors, according to Ephesians 4:8, 11

(KJV) are revered as being gifts from God to the church for distinct purposes of maturing the Saints, doing the work of ministry, and edifying the body of Christ (Ephesians 4:12, KJV). Therefore, effective pastors must be spiritual leaders endorsed by God, and their work extends far beyond rituals and ceremonies to change the lives of wayward people through the power, authority, and ability given through the Holy Spirit. That is why in the age of crises and crisis management, there is this critical need for spiritual men of God to answer this 3:00 a.m. wake-up call to the church. It is an urgent response required of spiritual men who have accepted the call of God to lead the church. It is time for spiritual men to stand up and be seen as men of God, speak out to be heard as the Voice of God, show the world that they are excited, and are not ashamed to do the work of God.

It is important to both believers and unbelievers, and

necessary for all that wrestle with problems, grief, agony, and despair that through spiritual leadership the church gets involved in this people changing, life-altering, heart touching process. It is a spiritual necessity for mending broken lives; even though life is a daily struggle for many people. It is a dog-eat-dog world with often the big dog walking away with the bone. People are being beaten up and beaten down in their everyday environments. They are looking for something to save them, revive them, and direct them. For these everyday warriors fighting against this evil world's system, Sunday is a day of relief, a time for spiritual renewal and hope that tomorrow will be better.

On Sunday morning, this day! The Lord's Day! Church people gather together in the Lord's house to seek and receive spiritual bliss. Because throughout the week, they've encountered personal attacks, hard trials, and many other negative occurrences that challenged their faith and motivation to remain Christian-minded outside the church walls. That's why on this holy day, inside these hallowed, sacred, spirit-filled walls, they don't want to fight. They don't want to see a fight. They don't want to be caught up in a fight. They want the security of being in God's house. They've come to church to worship God, feel His presence, and go home. They want the spiritual assurance that when they get to church, the Spirit of the Lord will be in the church! They want church pastors and church leaders to abandon carnal conflicts and walk together in the Spirit of Christ.

However, the truth of the matter is that in many places the church has lost its power to influence members to be excited about God. This shortage of enthusiasm for the church must be, in part, attributed to spiritual leaders that have lost connection with God. These spiritual leaders, which surrender to worldly positions, have forgotten their God-given assignments. They have become weak in their ability to provide strong, righteous spiritual leadership.

Weak spiritual leadership contributes greatly to the negative participation of members in church worship and church activities. The absence of sound doctrinal teachings that explains clearly and simply the church: its mission, purpose, and role, has resulted in much confusion in the church. Weak spiritual leadership hurts the church by allowing other church leaders to use rituals, laws, bylaws, and religious practices to gain church power. What about grace? God's grace! That is why, for some, the worship of God has become nothing more than a calculating litany; cold and lifeless worship services that leave worshippers hungering and thirsting for righteousness. With disappointment replacing praise many worshippers suffer through service after service. They know something is missing!

Creating the kind of atmosphere in churches where spiritual worship can take place to require spiritual leaders who love God, love the people, and love the fellowship of the Spirit. In the life of the church, honesty, devotion, and the desire to have God's will performed in the hearts of believers must be the objective of spiritual leaders. This process simply means getting back to the basics of church worship: let God be in everything, and everything be about God. There is therefore much work to be done, and spiritual leaders must give their undivided attention and spiritual concern for their work. Too often in their sincere desire to praise the Lord, many people enter the church to worship but leave not sure whether they have had a worship experience at all. When this occurs, members question within themselves, where is the spiritual leadership we need to grow? Where is the God that's not heard in the voice of the trumpet? Why doesn't the preacher speak with fervent spirit in his heart?

It is important for the spiritual health, growth, and development of the church that spiritual leaders assigned to the church desire to be spiritual leaders for the church, and in the church. Spiritual leaders that embrace their positions will more likely be effective and successful in their assigned ministry that often includes spiritual challenges, barriers, disappointments, as well as oppositions. Nevertheless, spiritual leaders are keepers of the sacred calling of the church and are responsible for leading and feeding the flock of God. Therefore, spiritual leaders must demonstrate their spiritual relationship and faith in God by the way they live, walk and talk.

The spiritual attitude, the spiritual altitude, and the spiritual worship atmosphere among church congregations usually indicate the spiritual depth of the people, and reflection of the spiritual leaders' effectiveness. The faith and growth of spiritual leaders will determine the spiritual interest and concerns of congregations they serve. As Christian congregations grow in their knowledge of God, and their spiritual relationship with God, it becomes possible for them to grasp the vision and become willing followers of their spiritual leaders.

Often, I've heard members of our church that have visited other churches come back with nothing but praise about their great worship experiences. They talked about the excitement and fulfillment they felt during the worship services. They sounded overjoyed with what they heard, observed, and received in the services; the spiritual singing of the choirs, and the powerful and inspiring sermons from the preachers they heard. However, at the same time, when they speak of or compare the same elements of worship that are practiced at our church services, the excitement levels from them go down, and the enthusiasm is lost. The explanation given by them for the differences is that our worship service is repetitive and lacks spiritual excitement. However, on the other hand, we've had people come to worship with us from other churches, and when they leave express appreciation and excitement about our worship services. What a difference perspective makes on what we see, receive, and believe. How is it that people that are passing by or visiting leave with one impression of church worship, while the people who come to the same church each week seem to lose appreciation for the worship they give? What are the two perspectives revealing or saying to us? Could the answer be as simple as desiring spiritual enrichment and fulfillment? On this Christian journey, and in this spiritual warfare, Christians need spiritual fire. The kind of spiritual fire that comes through Sunday morning worship services spiritually motivated by the presence of God through the Holy Spirit.

The Bible tells of a religious teacher named Nicodemus, who went to see Jesus by night and had to decide whether he was willing to be identified with Him or against Him. Nicodemus was a man with religious and civil status in his community. He was a busy man and had little time to waste on small issues or trivial matters. His day began early and often ended late in the evenings. He was a busy man. An important teacher. A great religious leader. Yet, after a full day's work, doing many things, and going many places, at the end of the day, he felt that something was missing in his life. He was searching for a way to fill the spiritually empty life he lived. He needed something or someone greater than what he had or what he was doing. He was looking for a spark, but what he found in his time with Jesus was the awareness that a change in heart will cause a spark of religious interest to become a spiritually burning fire.

CHAPTER 16
THE SPARK AND THE FIRE

Nicodemus was a Jewish priest, a Rabbi, and a member of the Sanhedrin Council, the ruling religious government of the Jewish people. He taught the people according to the laws God gave Moses. He earned the status of being a master teacher at his craft, and he practiced it with pride and integrity. In the gospel according to John, the beloved disciple of Jesus, he tells how Nicodemus' interest in Jesus caused him to leave the safety of his religious setting to seek a spiritual spark for his own life. Nicodemus had realized that the law could only take the seeker so far before it reached its limits. This limitation left the seeker with the need to touch God in a more personal relationship. Nicodemus knew the law. He knew that it was a guide to point the way to God. He knew that the law was good, but he also knew that the law did not fill the spiritual emptiness of his heart. The law, by itself, was not complete enough to fill the spiritual void. It was good work but not a final work. It was a leading process, but not a fulfilling process. Nicodemus knew and taught that the strength of the law was in its ability to set guidelines and enforce boundaries. As strict as the law was, the law keepers were not rewarded, but the lawbreakers were punished.

Somewhere along the way Nicodemus heard about Jesus and was interested in what He taught. Unlike the law, which only pointed the way to God, Jesus' teachings spoke of God as someone that can be personally known. It was more about a relationship with God than the practice of religious rituals. The teachings of Jesus were plain and simple. Everyone who had ears to hear could understand what he was saying. Jesus used materials to which the people could relate to describe the Kingdom of God. Even when

He talked about heaven, it was clear that He knew something about the place. This intrigued Nicodemus because the law had become nothing more than a stale legalistic companion that demanded more than it gave. The law was cold and indifferent because it had no passion, no life. Nicodemus knew that something was missing, and he needed a spiritual spark for his own spiritual life.

We are not told in the narrative why Nicodemus came to Jesus by night. We are left to draw our conclusions or rationales. Let me offer a few reasons of my own. One could be that it may have been the best time for him to get some "alone time" with Jesus. Remember, throughout His ministry days, Jesus was constantly surrounded by a multitude of people. This made it difficult for someone like Nicodemus to find isolated time with Him. Another reason Nicodemus came by night could have been that it was the only time Nicodemus had available at the end of a busy day performing his religious duties. We do not know for sure why he chose this time to seek Jesus, but we do know that he came to Jesus at night. He did not say it or even admit it, but we know that he needed a divine spark in his spiritual life.

The intimate spiritual relationship he was searching for could not be found in any of the synagogues in which he lectured or performed the ceremonial rituals. No matter how many temples he visited, they were all the same. They only offered him what he already had, emptiness. They only taught him what he already knew, the law. Hungry and desperate for a greater understanding of the spiritual life, Nicodemus talked with Jesus. We do not know for sure, but perhaps he thought that a quick visit with Jesus would provide a spiritual spark that would cause him to look more intently into the Law he coveted, taught, and practiced all his life. Perhaps he would discover some stimulating life in it that had been overlooked. Perhaps he thought that spending a little time with Jesus would confirm in his heart and mind that the Law was the right track to be on in life and that it was stronger and more enduring than some new religion that was nothing more than a passing movement. Whatever Nicodemus' initial motivation for coming to Jesus was, it did not matter, because once in the presence of the Lord, everything for him changed. Nicodemus wanted a spark. Jesus knew that he needed a fire.

Nicodemus thought flattery was a way to get the conversation started, but Jesus did not waste words. He knew that Nicodemus' concerns were spiritual. He told Nicodemus that what he needed was to be born again. Nicodemus did not understand how a man at his age could be born again. He could not reenter his mother's womb and be born. Nicodemus was locked into the natural, able to understand only what could be reasoned or explained. Nicodemus asked, "How could this happen?" Jesus told him that that which is flesh is flesh and that which is Spirit is Spirit. Jesus explained to him that understanding the new birth logically is like trying to grasp the wind. He told Nicodemus that no one could tell where the wind comes from or where it goes. It is the same way with the Spirit.

Nicodemus came for a spark, but when he left, he was on fire. We do not get proof of this change in Nicodemus' life until Jesus is crucified for the sins of the world. On the cross of Calvary, Jesus was executed as a criminal. His death was the price for man's sin. His sacrifice was man's redemptive salvation. He willingly suffered this humiliating death until He had accomplished everything that His Father asked of Him, and then He died. It was Nicodemus along with another secret disciple, Joseph of Arimathea, which asked Governor Pilate for the slain body of the Savior so that they could give him a proper burial. They took Jesus and buried Him in Joseph's new tomb (John 19:38-40).

There are many others like Nicodemus who think that they only need a spark to stir up their spiritual fervor, but what every believer need is the spiritual fire of the Lord burning deep in the heart. This fervor in the heart is the passionate desire of believers to share the good news of God's love with those searching for a relationship with God. When church people get excited about who God is and the life, He offers the world, it becomes too much to keep trapped between the sacred walls of the church. It is good news that needs to be passed on to those who have not heard it. Kurt Kaiser's song, "Pass It On," speaks volumes of how important it is to pass on your faith and love for God. He reminds the church that "It only takes a spark to get a fire going and soon all those around can warm up in its glowing. That's how it is with God's love once you've experienced it. You spread His love to everyone, you want to pass it on."

CHAPTER 17
ABRAHAM, THE FRIEND OF GOD

The faith of our fathers has become for the church, the foundation of our faith in God. What we know of God is given to us in the Word of God. Historically, our understanding of God has come to us down through the ages in hymns, spiritual writings, and sacrificial testimonies. It is our fathers' relationships with God, and their shared experiences of faith in God, that have allowed church members to believe in God, and take hold of trust, hope, and dependence on the invisible God. Through faith in God's word, He became alive in them, and that same faith has made Him alive in us. The life of the Christian church is made known to the world through spiritual witnessing for the Lord. The church is to present a clear message, filled with love, hope, and salvation to all who will believe it and receive it. The Christian church walks by faith in the face of a world of doubts. It has always been a faith walk. When the concept of a church or a people to worship God was conceived in God, He decided to establish a people of faith in the world that would bear His name and share His fellowship. Such a people would be uniquely linked to Him and known to the world as the people of God. For God to establish such a people He first had to have a man of faith that He could invest in, shape, mold, focus, and then trust to model that faith relationship. Such a man was named Abram, who lived in a country called Ur of the Chaldees. A land that practiced polytheism, the worship of many gods. At the call of Jehovah, the true and living God, this man took his wife, cattle, and other property and moved from the land of his father to go where God would lead him. It was not a business deal that moved him. It was this new relationship with the true and living God that directed his steps. It was his faith in God that caused him to walk away from the religious practices he knew and embraced a faith new to his relationship and belief in God.

Abram became known as the friend of God because he established a close relationship with God. He believed in God. He trusted God. Because of Abram's faith, God made him two specific promises that could only be received by faith. The first promise God made to him was that Abram would become the father of many nations. He was told that one day his descendants would be more in numbers than the stars in the sky or the sands on the seashore. The second promise was that He would give Abram a land filled with milk and honey. He was told that when he got there, everywhere his feet touched would be his land. Although those were good-sounding promises, Abrams had two problems with them. One, he had no directions to this

Promised Land, as to where it was located. It was a faith movement of going not knowing. Second, he and his wife Sarai were old and did not have any children of their own. How could he have multiple descendants? Despite these natural problems, he spiritually took God at His word and moved forward by faith. Along the way, God changed his name from Abram which means "A high father," to Abraham which means "father of a multitude." God also changed Abraham's wife's name from Sarai, which means "My princess" to Sarah, which means "princess for all the races." Abraham and Sarah walked by faith on their journey to the Promised Land.

Abraham spiritually led his family and servants to a relationship with God. He was effective in his witness because they could see by his action that God was the guiding force in his life. Likewise, the church today needs good spiritual examples of faith and strong spiritual leaders that will inspire and encourage believers to follow God. In some awakening ways, today's spiritual leaders need to be reminded of what it is that they are called to do, and that leadership is about trust. Abraham was the kind of man that God could trust. He was called by God out of a pagan world and placed on a spiritual journey of faith that would not only benefit him but the whole world. Building a spiritual nation on the faith of a man and his demonstrated ability to be trusted with that which is precious could not be more highlighted than when God tested Abraham.

After God kept His promise and gave Abraham and Sarah a son in their old ages, Abraham was one hundred and Sarah was ninety years old. God told Abraham to take Isaac, his only "spiritual son" Isaac, and give him back to God as a sacrificial offering (Genesis 22:1-14). Abraham did not hesitate. He prepared Isaac for the sacrifice. He was ready and willing to carry out God's command and had it not been for the voice of God that forbade him to perform the ritual, he would have offered his son on the altar for God. Abraham passed the test. It was not a test for God because God knows all. It was Abraham's test. Who do you love most? Abraham, by his action, demonstrated his love for God and proved that he could be trusted with what God gave him. It was Abraham's faith that began the building of a people who would serve God and be called children of the "Most High God." Abraham demonstrated a passionate faith in God that caused him to keep God's commands and God's guidance at the top of his priorities list. He was God's friend and he valued that friendship so highly that he would not jeopardize it with anything that was not pleasing to God.

It was his passion to do the will of God that allowed him to have this kind of spiritual intimacy with God.

CHAPTER 18
MEN GOD TRUSTED

Throughout human history, God has sought spiritual leaders, such as Abraham, who could be trusted with spiritual things. From the beginning, God emphasized the importance of spiritual trust. When Adam was created God trusted Adam's judgment and ability to give names and identities to every creature and living thing. Along with his daily chores, Adam was trusted to live in and care for his perfect home, the Garden of Eden. In this spiritual relationship, God established a communication line connecting God and man and the spiritual trust between God and Adam. Spiritual trust, like spiritual intimacy, is about having God in your heart and worshipping Him because you love Him. God placed a great responsibility on Adam's shoulders, and Adam proved to God that he could be trusted. A world of trust was placed in this man named Adam.

Moses was another man God trusted. He was the man of the hour at a time when God's people had lost their identity and spiritual relationship with God. God called Moses from his self-imposed exile in a desert country called Midian where he worked tending sheep for his father-in-law Jethro. God spoke to Moses from a burning bush and sent him to lead His people from a place of physical captivity and spiritual bondage to a place in the wilderness where they could worship Him. Moses was trusted with the task to faithfully and patiently lead an imprisoned nation of people to freedom and direct them to follow God. The problem for Moses, at this time, was that God's people had forgotten Him. They lacked the faith to believe in God, as well as how to worship and trust God during their captivity. Yet Moses was given the responsibility of delivering them spiritually and physically. The task was a difficult one for Moses because, among the people of God, some were stubborn, stiff-hearted, and determined to be disobedient. The continuous complaining and open rebellion against leadership eventually got to Moses. For a brief moment, this contentious spirit caused Moses to lose focus of what God told him to do. The people were thirsty and God told Moses to speak to the rock and he would get water. In his disgust of dealing with this bunch of ingrates, he did not follow God's instruction for getting water from the rock. God told Moses to take his rod and assemble the people at the rock and speak to the rock and the water would flow. Instead of speaking to the rock, Moses struck the rock twice. His act of the flesh cost him a trip to the Promised Land (Numbers 20:8-13). Moses was given a difficult task, an almost impossible task.

How do you lead people on a spiritual journey when they are carnal-minded? How do they worship the living God when they do not know God? Nevertheless, God gave the people water from the rock and blessed Moses for his leadership. For more than 300 years of enslavement, fear, and punishment through fear, these people had been conditioned to honor and please the pharaohs who made themselves to be gods. However, when freedom came through Moses it was difficult for many of the slaves to embrace this new life because freedom was something they did not know, and had not experienced. Although they were free and on their way to the Promised Land, when faced with the first, of many challenges of the journey, getting across the Red Sea, some were ready to give up and go back into slavery rather than going forward into freedom.

Pharaoh changed his mind about setting the Israelites free and sent his soldiers to return them to slavery. Such actions brought renewed fear to this newly delivered crowd and drowned the enthusiasm of freedom that had been birthed in the hearts of these people. The fear they had towards their captors was greater in them than their faith in God, who they did not know. It appeared to them that they were trapped on every side and were surely destined to die right there. The obstacles and barriers that trapped them offered them no hope for survival. The mountains were at their sides, the army at their backs and the Red Sea prevented their forward progress. This faithless crowd of God complained to Moses and accused him of bringing them out there to die. The thinking of this crowd was that it would have been better for them back in Egypt as slaves rather than being trapped in this hopeless predicament. Moses, the lawgiver, was perplexed himself. He believed that God sent him to deliver the people from bondage. Yet, why was God not helping him? When he needed God most, where was He? God calmed Moses' doubts and assured him that everything that he needed to accomplish his task was with him. God told Moses to simply stretch out his rod. When Moses trusted the Word of God, a miracle took place.

The Red Sea opened up and dried up so that the people were able to cross over on the dry ground and marched on toward the Promised Land. The same fate was not afforded by Pharaoh's army, which tried to follow God's people without God's approval. They drowned in the Red Sea and were no longer a persecuting threat to the people of God. God's people were delivered and placed on a path that would lead them to their spiritual identity and their spiritual greatness. Through his demonstrated faith and actions Moses was a spiritual example of the kind of man God trusts to get the job done.

There was still another man that God trusted in establishing His spiritual kingdom. His name was David. He was introduced to us as a shepherd boy who as a faithful worker cared for his father's sheep, cattle and protected them from wild beasts (I Samuel 16:11). Later we learned of his courage when he stood up to a giant named Goliath and defeated him. Goliath challenged the people of God for a champion to fight him. David stood up to this giant of a man when all others were afraid to do so (I Samuel 17:32-37). Then we learned that David was both loyal and faithful. Saul, the king of Israel, honored David for his courage but hated him because of his popularity. When the people sang

David's praises, King Saul became envious and bitter toward him and eventually forced David to run and hide for his life. David remained loyal to the king and respected his office despite all the troubles that Saul heaped on him. Although Saul tried to kill David and could not, David had many occasions to kill Saul and would not. David was faithful to God and would not touch or do harm to King Saul, God's anointed office holder. He had faith that God would protect him, and deliver him at the right time. God had anointed David to be king and David trusted God. In God's time, David was crowned king over the people of God. He had courage, patriotic pride, and a heart for God. Through his relationship with God David was promised that a king would sit on his throne forever. He was trusted with a dynasty. Just as important as David's relationship with God and his leadership of God's people were then, so is the need of the church today for spiritual leaders who are trustworthy, loyal, and faithful.

Last, but certainly not least, Jesus was a man that God trusted then, now, and always. The unique task given Him to perform was one that only He could accept and accomplish. His job was to restore a world lost in darkness back to an enlightened spiritual relationship with God. A relationship that had been broken by sin and separated man from God. His assignment required a loving heart, a willing spirit, and a perfect sacrifice. Jesus was in a spiritual position to carry out this distinct work because unlike all other men before Him, a disobedient Adam, a dishonest Abraham, a strident Moses, a covetous David, and many others, Jesus had no flaws, failures, or faults. During His ministry years, Jesus modeled the image of God before a world that had religiously re-made God in their image. Jesus, however, was different.

Everything He did was different from the religious practices that held the people in spiritual bondage. Although He did not come into the world to change the law or the prophets, he came to make them complete (Matthew 5:17), His differences gave life to either dead or worn-out rituals and procedures. He made a difference in the life of men, whether He opened the eyes of the blind or cured incurable diseases, or simply provided a spiritually encouraging word (Luke 4:18). When He spoke to the people about what God saw in them, love could be heard in what He said. When He taught them about God, the people could envision Heaven from the pictures He painted (John 14:2-3). When He ministered to the helpless, hurting, and rejected, the people could see and feel the joy of belonging to and knowing God personally (Mark 5:18-19). Jesus did His work well and He made a spiritual difference. For three years Jesus took personal delight in His work as He taught ordinary men, His disciples, to become spiritual leaders in the kingdom of God.

Making disciples was His goal. To accomplish this task His work was most challenging. He chose twelve men to invest in spiritual training and teach them how to give away their faith. It took exceptional spiritual skills to mold and shape such a diverse bunch of men whose different perspectives of life did not naturally put them together into a spiritual team. How could you expect an ordinary person with natural abilities to blend an effective spiritual team that would turn the world upside down? A team consisting of uneducated fishermen, cheating tax collectors, an overzealous radical, along with other professions of men not revealed in scriptures? Will they listen to and take spiritual guidance from a carpenter's son who claims to be God's Son? This cannot be done effectively unless God is in it. It must be a God thing! It took a God-man to get it done. Jesus finished His work on the cross at Calvary.

Before He took His final breath, He acknowledged to the Father that He had done what He had come to do, that is, to be the sacrificial offering for sin. It appeared to all who witnessed the crucifixion that an end had occurred. A ministry, a movement, or a passing in the night operation, whatever it was, appeared over with as a defeated Jesus hung on the cross. However, three days later a victorious Jesus rose from the grave with the declaration that all power was in His hand. Out of Jesus' sacrifice for the world man was given another opportunity to have fellowship with God. Because of God's great love for the world, mankind can now have and share in a new life, a new hope, and a new faith in God. Jesus' commitment to His assigned task caused Him to fulfill His work. He was and is a man that God trusted and will trust.

There is a need today in the life of the church for men and women to be spiritually renewed and positioned to be used for the glory of God. It comes down to people being in love with God and the church. Church members everywhere need to fall in love with God all over again. It is hard to overlook or ignore people who are in love. Love is being alive. Love is energetic. Love is getting involved and making it count. Love's electricity lights up wherever it is shared. The actions of people in love are evident by the quality and quantity of time invested in the relationship. When people are in love, they take pride in how they look, careful in what they say, and are concerned about the images they project. When you are in love with the church you make sure that all things are done decently and in order. Such people work diligently to ensure that the atmosphere of the church is filled with the fragrance of love and all who inhale it are spiritually renewed in their walk with the Lord.

PART IV

CHAPTER 19
CONCLUSION

Passion is the fuel that energies love, life, and spiritual intimacy. When was the last time you found yourself doing something that you enjoyed doing? Was it at work? Perhaps it was a hobby you have reserved for spare times! Has your heart been totally into you doing your daily activities? Have you given your best today? Questions such as these challenge our interests, motivations, desires, and require courage from within to demand that each day we get the most out of the lives we live. Therefore, you need passion to enjoy the life you live, the work you do, and the relationships you treasure. When passion is your energy, all that you do will reflect a relentless effort to achieve the highest and the best. When passion is the partner that you choose to pursue your dreams and goals, adventure, excitement, and fulfillment will be the benefit of your motivation.

The purpose of this writing was an effort to identify and highlight people with the courage and passion to live their lives doing what they love doing. These were common people, everyday people, and spiritual people who've worked hard at their tasks and still had joy doing it. Passion, which is more than a concept, empowers each day, in the lives of these people, to be filled with enthusiasm, and anticipation of greater opportunities to improve. Once the kind of passion that elevates spiritual thinking has been embraced in the heart, its kind of love will dissolve into pleasure that assures having joy in doing the work we do. Passion strengthened the life from emptiness as it rekindles, restores, and reenergizes all that make their journey a quest for completion.

CHAPTER 20
VESTAL GOODMAN AND SQUIRE PARSONS

Recently, while watching a Bill Gaither gospel video, I noticed the diversity in the singers that were on stage together. They were there, old and young, men and women, grouped singing praises to the glory of God. It was a shared journey of passionate singing of songs they loved singing. Delight could be seen on all their faces. It was evident that they liked what they were doing. Ms. Vestal Goodman, a veteran southern gospel singer, led a song that inspired and motivated the others to join in the singing. It was evident, from the first to the last note of the song, the joy of the song came from her heart. Her expressions and gestures amplified the message that she liked what she was doing.

Squire Parsons, another prominent gospel singer, was one of the many participants on that stage. As he sang

"Sweet Beulah Land," one of his most recognized songs, you could feel the passion that brought the words of the song to life. His passion revealed in this rendition of the song indicated that his heart was in it, and it meant something to him. His expressions told me that he liked what he was doing. What makes these soldiers of God's musical army continue to sing to the glory of God years after the height of their popularity has faded? What caused them to still smile when the name of Jesus flowed from their lips? What motivated them to sing another song even at times they were tired? The answer is simple. They have the passion to like what they do and do what they like doing with passion.

CHAPTER 21
BOBBY COX

The story of Bobby Cox, the former baseball manager of the Atlanta Braves, was another person that recently caught my attention. He was a leader with a great passion for both the game he played and the successful manager he became. His leadership approach and preparation for a baseball season were awe-inspiring. After more than 20 years as a manager in the game, and of the Atlanta Braves his enthusiasm for the game remained high, intense, and enjoyable for him. During his time and tenure as the Atlanta Braves manager, he had some disappointing years wherein the team finished either at or near the bottom of their divisions. Many managers lacking this passion for the game would have quit and tried some other career before they were fired, but not Bobby Cox. He was determined to succeed, and make his team the winners they were destined to become. The 1990 baseball season ended with the Braves at the bottom of their division. Another disappointing baseball season! Leaving to be answered the question or doubtful expectation, will next season be any better? The passion for effective leadership would provide the qualifying answer. That is the 1991 baseball season was a complete turnaround for the Atlanta Braves. This team, led by manager Bobby Cox, went from being worst to first in their division. The Atlanta Braves, America's team, for thirteen straight years, through his leadership, were crowned division champions. A few of those years they were league champions, and one of those years they became world champions. Bobby Cox, manager of the Atlanta Braves, had a passion for what he was doing. He liked shaping young players into great players. He had a passion for the game.

CHAPTER 22
MY FRIEND ALBERT

My dear friend Albert is a local mechanic with a deep passion for doing mechanical works. He loves working on cars. He was once regarded as a top-of-the-line mechanic, but now he works on cars as a sideline specialist. He has expert knowledge in how to fix and repair mechanically impaired vehicles. He knows his craft. Years ago, Albert worked for a national automobile corporation as a highly qualified mechanic. His mechanical expertise had promoted and positioned him to attain higher responsibilities and recognitions as a mechanic when, without warning, he became ill, and his failed health forced him to leave his job. All was going well for him until he became ill and was no longer able to do his job. Although his health issue caused him to leave the workplace, it did not stop him from doing what he had the passion for doing, fixing cars. His reputation and skilled work as a quality mechanic kept people coming to him to care for their vehicles. Albert loved it. No matter what time of the day or evening, he was just a phone call away, ready to fix cars here and there.

He was going along getting satisfaction out of helping people and working on cars when a second attack on his health occurred. He was at a high school seniors' award event for his son when it hit him. Albert collapsed from a brain aneurysm that placed him in the hospital in a coma for more than two weeks. His condition was dire. His potential for recovery seemed remote. The picture of restored life and abilities didn't appear possible for Albert. The medical staff did not give him much of a chance for recovery, and if he did, he would require at least a year of rehabilitation.

Albert defied that prognosis. Miraculously, after being in the hospital for two weeks, with the expectations that he might be there a much longer time, he unexpectedly woke up one morning with praises to God on his lips. At first, his memory was sporadic, but soon afterward he was able to regain his memory. Albert was a miracle. Contrary to what he was told not to do by friends and family about taking it easy, and staying away from any mechanical works, a few days after he had gotten out of the hospital, Albert was back diagnosing cars, and in a limited way, fixing cars. To many people who were concerned about his health it seemed an unwise move for him to be out trying to work on cars; but for Albert, working on cars was both therapeutic, and a healing process. It may not have been what others would have him do, but for Albert, he was doing what he liked doing. It was his passion that made him do it and keeps doing it.

CHAPTER 23
JOCQUELINE

Recently, at a church event, I saw a very special Christian woman immersed in her skill as a leader of music and inspiring in her task as a teacher of songs to young people. Her name is Jocqueline Richardson. "Joc" to those who know her best. She is a woman of music and a lady of songs. Her passion is a musical story. She is an educator and a professional music teacher. During most of her career, she worked as a high school music teacher training and developing young voices to become great singers. After many years of teaching and training students' voice and music lessons in public schools, she moved to the college level where she continued teaching students through her musical skills, knowledge, and expertise.

Her years teaching in the public school system were

valued times of positive interactions which greatly impacted numerous students' lives and potential musical careers. Throughout her school years-time, she untiringly and passionately invested herself in her work and her students. Annually, she prepared her chorus students to perform their musical and vocal skills, at the school concert, to their highest levels of performance.

Her musical passion accompanied her Christian faith and she applied it as the music and choir director in her local church. She, with passionate musical skills to instruct and develop the church choirs, which consisted of ordinary people who loved to sing, into glorious-sounding voices that gave praises to God. In addition to working in the local church, Ms. Richardson, as she is respectfully addressed, makes herself available to work in the music department at the district, wing, and state levels of the Alabama State

Missionary Baptist Convention. At each level, she skillfully, professionally, and passionately incorporated the voices, personalities, and vocal skills of young people from various locations across the state, by merging their voices into vocal harmony to ready them to present them before the parent body of the convention.

Oh yeah, did I point out the fact that this has to be done in hours rather than days? That's right! Ms. Richardson, like Houdini with a baton, applied her skills to teach young people to sing the requested songs to the glory of God. And she did it again and again; year after year to the same level of proficiency and excellence. She is an extraordinary woman that loves music. She has music in her heart. The main reason that she does so much with music is that she likes what she does and she does it with passion. Musical passion! Symphonic passion! Lover of voices with potential greatness passion! God, in her heart passion! For more than 40 years she has dedicated her life to music. Music is in her thinking. Music fills her day. Music is in her heart. Music is she. Music is her passion!

CHAPTER 24
FINAL THOUGHTS

Life matters! Every life is a precious indication of potential greatness, contributions, and the pursuit of happiness. Therefore, life, being too short to take for granted, must be examined each day for personal security, fulfillment, and the passion by which to live it. That is why it is essentially important for everyone not to settle for a lifestyle that drains the energy of existence from your purpose, but rather with determined passion and courage, persevere to do what you like doing. Life is too valuable of an impact on the world to spend it doing things that you hate, regret, or simply not want to do it. The time has come for all who are unhappy with their lives, or the work they do, to turn those frowns into smiles, sadness into gladness, and nightmares into dreams by making efforts to do what they like doing and want to do. Therefore, secure your dreams! The life you live must be big enough for you to trust your heart to someone you love without fear that it will be broken. It must be big enough for you to invest it in a profession, a job, a skill, or the work that you like doing because it has meaning to you. You must not let doubts and discouragements keep you from reaching for success. It must be big enough to allow the spiritual intimacy that you have with God to direct your works for God.

ABOUT THE AUTHOR

Rev. (Dr.) Lorenza James has served as pastor of Tabernacle Missionary Baptist Church, Tuscaloosa, Alabama since 1995. He is a graduate of The University of Alabama (BA), American Intercontinental University (M.Ed.), and Northcentral University (Ed. D.). He is a veteran of the U.S. Army attaining the active duty rank of Captain. His love for God, church, and people has been the primary motivation and passion for writing this book.